See Sally
Kick Ass

A Woman's Guide
to Personal Safety

By Fred Vogt

Outskirts Press, Inc.
Denver, Colorado

See Sally Kick Ass
A Woman's Guide to Personal Safety
All Rights Reserved
Copyright © 2007 Fred Vogt

Outskirts Press
http://www.outskirtspress.com

ISBN-10: 1-59800-820-X
ISBN-13: 978-1-59800-820-3

Outskirts Press and the "OP" logo are trademarks belonging to
Outskirts Press, Inc.

Printed in the United States of America

Disclaimer

This book intends to provide ideas on how to prevent and avoid becoming a crime victim. Every situation in which you encounter a criminal is different. You must make the decision on what to do about a specific situation at the time it occurs. Neither FKV Enterprises LLC nor the author make any representation, warranty or guarantee that the ideas and techniques described or illustrated in this book will be safe or effective in any confrontation or otherwise. The ideas in this book may not work in every instance. Use of these ideas does not guarantee that you will not sustain injury or property loss. You may be injured or injure others if you apply or train in the use of the self-defense techniques described or illustrated in this book. Neither FKV Enterprises LLC nor the author is responsible for any injuries that may result. The reader should apply only the force that is reasonable to respond appropriately to the situation. The reader is cautioned to be knowledgeable of the federal, state and local laws with regard to self-defense. Use of excessive force or any degree of force not justifiable under the circumstances at hand may be a crime or give rise to civil liability on the part of the actor. Neither FKV Enterprises LLC nor the author make any representations or warranty regarding the legality or appropriateness of any technique or idea mentioned in this book.

Dedication

With love to my wife and our daughters.

Acknowledgements

Writing a book for the first time is always a challenge. Many people gave me assistance along the way making the job much easier. I would like to thank my wife and daughters for providing continuous encouragement and support. They provided many suggestions and experiences along with editorial review. My mother, age 90, had input on keeping the elderly safe. Sensei Michael Black, The Woodlands Aikido Center, The Woodlands, Texas, and Sensei Elliot Freeman of Three Rivers Aikido, St. Louis, Missouri, provided insight into self-defense techniques and helped broaden my understanding of aikido. Sensei Dr. Frank Gallo, Rhode Island Aikido, Cranston, Rhode Island, helped with technical assistance. Susan Lawrence and Laura Landsbaum served as my very much appreciated editors. Joel B. Daniels, Attorney at Law, helped further my understanding of the legal issues surrounding self-defense. I want to thank my photographic models, Sue, Lora, and Elliot, who helped illustrate the various self-defense techniques. I would also like to thank Outskirts Press for their professional help and assistance.

Table of Contents

Introduction

The smoke drifted up slowly from the dangling cigarette in the thin, hard mouth of the criminal as he hid in the shadows looking over the parking lot for his next victim. When would she come? Sounds like the opening to a book of fiction, but it's a real life scenario happening every day. This book is designed to help prevent *you* from becoming that next victim.

See Sally Kick Ass: A Woman's Guide to Personal Safety addresses the issue of personal safety for women in today's world. There was a time when you didn't have to lock your front door. There were no carjackings or date rape drugs. Times have changed. Now we not only lock our front door, but we also set our security alarms. The reality is that there is risk out there and that most women have not had any experience or training to enhance their personal safety. That's where this book comes in.

Why do I feel so passionately about the personal safety of women? I am married and have three daughters of my own. Not only would I like them to be able to go through life safely, but I also have that wish for *you* and all women. This book is my small contribution toward that goal. Being safe does not magically happen; each of you must be an active participant in your own personal safety program. This book will help arm you with ideas to enhance that program.

Crime occurs in all neighborhoods and to women of all walks of life. The goal of this book is to educate you in the *simple everyday precautions* that you can take to significantly reduce the likelihood that you will be involved in an adverse situation or become a victim. It does not require major changes to your lifestyle or doing things that are difficult. As a

1

matter of fact, most of these suggestions are common sense things that we should all be doing already. However, sometimes we need a reminder that these ideas should be part of our everyday habits.

Since my wife and daughters have had input on this book, I have used some of their experiences as a basis for some of the suggestions. One daughter is a marketing executive for a major corporation, the second currently is a homemaker with children, and the third has spent the last five years teaching in Southeast Asia and the Middle East. I have had very diversified input.

The focus of this book is primarily on prevention: how you can do small things that help reduce your risks and how not to be at the wrong place at the wrong time. However, there may be times when you do everything right and a confrontation still occurs. In those cases, this book describes how to use verbal self-defense to de-escalate or defuse the situation. If that fails, this book does teach specific woman-oriented self-defense techniques to help deal with would be attackers.

How about taking a martial arts class and just skip reading this book? Hint – reading this book is actually easier. Martial arts classes will teach you what to do when someone physically attacks you. Remember though, it's about *prevention,* not reaction. This is the part most martial arts classes leave out. Does that mean martial arts classes aren't good? No, not at all - those classes will help teach you what to do when someone attacks you and will make you more confident in handling a problem. I think any martial arts training will be good for you, but I think that you should do everything possible not to have to physically deal with a criminal. Prevention means not having to face an attacker. The point is this; try not to put yourself in the situation where you are forced to demonstrate your martial arts understanding. The focus should be on *prevention.*

While the emphasis is on prevention, you may find yourself being confronted. You should know that every situation is different, so there is no one standard answer. Making a decision means evaluating many factors: distance to safety, likelihood of a response to shouts of distress, type of weapon displayed, size of attacker, perceived strength, number of people threatening you, likelihood of persuading them to stop, your chance of defeating the individual with your self-defense skills, etc. This instantaneous evaluation will help you decide on fight or flight. Flight, if you can be successful, is always the better choice. If you have to fight as a last resort, then it is best to be prepared with some basic knowledge of techniques that will truly work for women. This book will not attempt to make you a black belt, but it will teach you basic skills that can be used to escape grasps and dissuade attackers.

The good news is that according to the U.S. Department of Justice, Bureau of Justice Statistics, the National Crime Victimization Survey (NCVS), crime has decreased since 1994 by about 50%. While that is great news, if you are a victim of a crime, the reduction rate is meaningless. You were still the victim of a crime. My objective is to help reduce the crime rate even further by making you a harder target and by preventing you from being involved in a criminal incident or becoming a victim.

This book contains lots and lots of ideas that at first glance may seem a little daunting. Many ideas may already be part of your daily life, others you can implement fairly easily and there will be some that might be difficult. Don't fret if you can't do each and every one. While any that you adopt will help reduce your risk, there are some that just may not work for you. This is meant as a guide or a suggestion list. Make as many as you can part of your everyday life. Periodically pull out this book and review the various ideas to see if they have truly become part of your routine habit and if there are others that you can now implement. I encourage you to mark up this book. Take a highlighter to it and earmark those pages that you find interesting.

Framework

The 4 A's of Personal Safety

Everyone has a personal safety plan. It is what you do, consciously or subconsciously, to reduce your risks on a daily basis. In some cases the plan may be fairly minimal, "I lock my doors." In other cases the plan has been carefully thought through with the various risk factors weighed against the cost of the prevention measures. In either case, there are probably simple things that can be done to further enhance your existing plan. Some of these you will be able to adapt easily and incorporate immediately while others may take more time.

The **4 A's** is a program I designed to prevent or reduce the probability that a woman will be involved in an "adverse situation." I define an "adverse situation" as having property taken from you or having physical harm come to you or your family. The program is focused on prevention. Ideally, you will never have to do deal with a criminal by having taken the appropriate preventative measures. Three of the **4 A's** discuss prevention while the fourth **A** is a response if prevention has failed. While the focus is primarily on prevention, taking direct action may prove to be necessary.

What are the **4 A's**?

Attitude - the mindset you have and the image you project.
Awareness – seeing what is going on around you.
Avoidance – simple everyday actions to reduce risk.
Action – direct steps to take when confronted.

We are going to delve into each of these **4 A's** to understand why they are important and how they fit together as part of your overall personal safety plan. While each **A** by itself is important, together they form a much stronger integrated plan. We will discuss not only your personal safety, but also your family's safety both at home and while traveling. Let's get started!

Chapter 1

Attitude

"Position or posture of the body appropriate to or expressive of an action, emotion, etc." – Random House Dictionary

Why is **Attitude** important? **Attitude** starts with you and your commitment to be an active part of enhancing your personal safety. Because you *can* reduce the probability of being involved in an "adverse situation," you can do simple things to substantially reduce your personal risk. You need to be involved in building layers of prevention and protection around yourself. Your plan should not be like an egg with one thin shell, but more like an onion with many layers. As you go through this book, mark those ideas that you currently don't do, but think you can implement as part of your personal safety program. Make a conscious commitment to start using them on a daily basis, like always locking the car doors. Once a month pull out this book and check your progress. The most important person in the equation is you.

Every day you see people and make visual judgments concerning their positions in life, wealth, emotional state, attractiveness, etc. Just as you are making assessments of other people, they are looking at you and making their own assessments. Why is understanding this really important? Criminals look for targets that appear weak, distracted or otherwise easy to subdue. They are looking for persons they consider to be vulnerable. When a criminal is looking for potential victims, you do not want to be perceived as the lowest person on the food chain.

What is the law of the jungle? The strong eat the weak or *perceived weak*. When the lion goes hunting, he is not looking for a difficult fight; he is looking for a weak victim for a quick meal. The lion also knows

7

that an injured predator quickly becomes prey, and therefore he must exercise a certain amount of caution. Now understand if a lion has no other choice, he will tackle even a difficult target, but that will not be his first choice. How does the law of the jungle impact you? The objective here is for *you* not to be perceived as weak or vulnerable.

We need to start at the beginning. A strong image starts with a positive mindset. Stand tall with an upright posture, head held high, looking forward. Slumping or letting your shoulders droop communicates weakness.

Fig. 1 Strong & ready   Fig. 2 Weak   Fig. 3 Distracted

If you were a criminal looking for an easy victim, which person would you target?

Fig. 4 Alert   Fig. 5 Ready – keys out   Fig. 6 Distracted

Walk with determination, with your head up, swinging your arms and exuding confidence. Project the image that you are alert and can deal with any issue that you have to face. Walk tall with your head up, looking around so that you are aware of everything in your surroundings. When you practice this, walking strong and exuding confidence will become part of your natural style helping perception become reality. Criminals can sense uncertainty or vulnerability, giving those people extra scrutiny. They can also sense confidence, which normally does not meet their definition of a good target.

Interestingly, people who have obtained black belts in martial arts get in fewer fights and confrontations than other people, why? I believe that black belts have more confidence and therefore subconsciously carry themselves differently. I can't tell you how I walk differently now that I am a black belt, but I do. Shortly after I got my first black belt, I was at the beach and came back to my car to find four guys drinking beer, with one of them perched on the hood of my car. I thought, "Great, I have to deal with four drunks." However, I did have absolute confidence that I could handle all four of them. When I politely asked the man to get off the hood of my car he said, "I'm sorry sir," and immediately got off. Now he might have gotten off the car anyway, but I believe my confident attitude had a lot to do with his quick response. Note that I politely asked him to get off my car and didn't call him

9

names or threaten him, which might have challenged his ego and caused him to respond differently.

When you are going from point A to point B, do not talk on your cell phone, wear headphones, read something or otherwise let yourself be distracted. Your job is to get safely from A to B. Treat that as your primary job and make the cell phone call later. If you do talk on your cell phone, make sure your head is up and you are looking left to right as you are talking. You always want to project a strong image that says you are alert. Criminals are looking for women that are distracted and not paying attention to what is going on around them. This allows them to get close to the potential victim and strike quickly.

Your image plays a key role in your perceived vulnerability. If you are confronted or a strange person approaches, do not stand with your feet side by side. Stand with one foot approximately 12 inches in front of the other, more of your weight on the front foot and leaning slightly forward. Martial artists call this a strong stance, projecting an image of readiness (see Fig. 7-8). Right away, your image says, "My system is on alert and ready." Criminals do not like "alert and ready" because they know that it will no longer be "quick and easy." "Alert and ready" will cause a criminal to reassess his plan and in many cases make him decide to find an easier target. Note in Fig. 8 how the hands are up and ready.

Fig. 7   Fig. 8

Several of my students have told me about incidents in which they believe by just projecting a strong image they were able to avoid an "adverse situation." They believe they projected a confidence about being able to handle the situation which caused the potential attacker to change his mind and go the other way. Think about that – just by projecting a strong image you can significantly reduce your probability of being a victim.

Let's review the key points for **Attitude**:

✓ You can reduce your risks by making simple changes to your everyday life.
✓ Stand with a positive upright posture and walk confidently.
✓ Use a strong stance if confronted.
✓ Exude confidence.
✓ Don't allow anything to distract you.
✓ Present a strong overall image.

Chapter 2

Awareness

"Having knowledge; conscious; cognizant: aware of the danger" – *Random House Dictionary*

W hy is **Awareness** important? You wouldn't step in a mud puddle or out in front of a car, so why go into dangerous situations? How does this happen? Because women today are very busy balancing all of the complex responsibilities in their lives, their own safety and awareness get lost in the shuffle. A woman can be distracted doing other tasks and suddenly find herself in a serious predicament. For example, a person in an automobile accident that says, "I didn't see the other car." Why not?

Many people own cats. There are "outside" cats, and there are cats that stay "inside" the house. These "inside" cats, when they are inside, are a picture of total relaxation, rubbing up against you, lounging on the sofa and generally taking life easy; they are the diva of the house. They don't have a care in the world. However, periodically these "inside" cats go outside. What happens? Watch them as they walk out of the door because as soon as they barely get outside they become very alert, ears perking up, looking side to side and all around. Why? Because they instinctively know they are in the danger zone, and they are looking for the dog! We can learn from these cats by becoming more aware of our surroundings.

All of you know about radar, which uses radio frequency pulses that reflect off targets to determine their distance. It is in everyday use to safely route airplanes and of course, catch the occasional person exceeding the speed limit. The radar dish that rotates sending out and receiving the pulses is a familiar sight. You need to adapt a similar scanning process to evaluate your surroundings.

I want you to be like the "inside" cat, being highly alert when going outside and to use your radar as you travel from one safe zone to the next. Safe zones generally are places like your home, your locked car, your office, shop or other building where there are people. Your job is to get safely between these zones, or from point A to point B.

As you exit a safe zone, use your radar and scan the area, looking left and right to see if anything looks unusual. Make it a practice to look side to side just like radar scanning the area you are entering. Is there someone lounging around your car? Is there a male sitting in the passenger seat in a car parked on the driver's side of your car? Continue to scan your surroundings after getting into your car. Does the same car keep showing up in your rear view mirror even after making several turns? Are there several men lounging at that street corner where it appears you will have to stop for a red light? All of these and many others should raise a red flag. However, if you identify a problem ahead of time, you can take action to avoid it.

You cannot do an adequate job of radar scanning if you are distracted. We all see many women with their heads down, either just walking or talking on their cell phones as they are strolling across parking lots, totally unaware of what is going on around them. The risk for these women has gone up substantially. They appear to be more vulnerable, and by their actions, the perception is that they are lower on the food chain. It is imperative that you be alert to potential problems. While I don't want you to be paranoid about going outside, I do want you to get in the habit of looking around and making it a routine action as you go about your everyday activities. How much more you actually see and are aware of by using the scanning techniques will surprise you. Just by looking around, you are communicating to anyone watching that you are alert and therefore not an easy target.

Being alert like an "inside" cat going outside and using your radar will help identify and prevent you from going into potentially dangerous situations. Not only will you be more likely to identify potential problems, but you will also project a stronger image by looking alert. A two for one!

Let's review **Awareness**:

✓ Don't be preoccupied with other tasks.
✓ Be like an "inside" cat when going outside.
✓ Look side to side and use your "radar."
✓ Make scanning part of your routine.

Chapter 3

Avoidance

"The act of keeping away from" – Random House Dictionary

The third **A** in our four step program is **Avoidance**. A problem never encountered is the best kind of problem. Here we want to identify simple, everyday things that can help avoid a problem developing. These are really common sense ideas that will help prevent you from becoming a potential victim. We'll start with ideas to enhance your safety at home and progress to other routine activities. Many of these suggestions might seem obvious, but they bear repeating.

The most important single item to enhance your personal safety is the cell phone. If you don't have one, get one for yourself and any teenager in your family. I consider it imperative. It can be used to call for assistance at any time and is absolutely worth the cost. It is cheap insurance to prevent problems. Program the cell phone with an ICE number which stands for "In Case of Emergency." Emergency personnel know to look for this number in your phone list, and they can notify someone of your situation.

Many prevention and avoidance ideas are going to be presented here. Mark those that you should be doing. Decide to start utilizing these ideas in your daily life. Some you can incorporate easily while others may take some time and effort, but these small steps could make a real difference in your life.

Residence

▪ When considering apartments, call local police and inquire about crime in that neighborhood and any problems at that complex.

Drive around at night to see the lighting. Document what the manager states about security. Put in writing any suggestions for improvements to security.

- A second or higher floor in apartment buildings is better than the first floor where there is easier access to windows.
- Treat apartment corridors as you would streets.
- Request 24 hour prior notice before anyone comes to your apartment for maintenance and insist that you receive written information concerning any time anyone enters your apartment for maintenance or any other reason stating who, when and why.
- Inquire how the apartment master key is controlled and if there are duplicate keys to your apartment. If there is a duplicate key for your apartment, put it in an envelope, writing your name on the back across the seal.
- Always change locks or have a locksmith change the tumblers and keying when you move into your new home or apartment. Don't be surprised by the last occupant that kept a key. Do not hide a spare key outside the front door. Criminals know to look over the door and under the door mat or flower pot. It is better to give a spare key to a trusted neighbor.
- When you have extra keys made, stand and watch each key being made. Do not leave because you want to be certain an extra key is not made. Pay in cash since a check or credit card can be used to get your address.
- Make sure there are deadbolts on exterior doors. Replace the short screws in the lock strike plates with longer 2.5 inch screws which will go into the jamb and not tear out easily (see Fig. 9). If you have a chain on the door, replace those short screws with longer screws.

Fig. 9 Inserting longer screw into strike plate

- Always keep ground floor windows closed.
- Make sure you have opaque curtains that when pulled cannot be seen through. Make sure curtains are pulled or blinds closed at night. Don't undress close to curtains where your silhouette might be seen.
- Put a deadbolt on your bedroom door.

- If you have wooden sash windows, you can further secure them by drilling a hole through the wooden framing around the glass of the window where the upper and lower parts of the sash overlap (see Fig. 10). The hole should be drilled at the upper corner of the sash on one side of the window. Measure carefully to drill a hole completely through the interior sash and halfway though the sash on the outside of the overlap. Place a two-headed nail or a small eye bolt into the hole making sure it is long enough to go into both frames. The two-headed nail or the eye on the bolt will allow you to withdraw it to open the window if necessary.

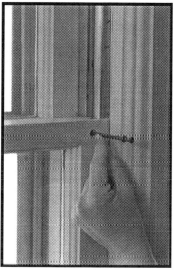

Fig. 10

- Cut a length of broomstick or dowel rod to lay in the track of a glass sliding door to prevent it from being opened. Cut it no more than 1/4 inch shorter than the door's opening. Tape or staple a short piece of string to the broomstick, making lifting it up out of the track easier. Screw a small screw into the upper track of the sliding door so that the door frame just misses it when opening or closing. This will keep the door from being lifted out of its track.
- Install a security system and outside motion detector lights. Even just security stickers on your windows will cause a criminal to sometimes hesitate and look for an easier target.

- Consider getting a dog since they can be a very good security system and a deterrent to potential criminals. Even a small dog works, it doesn't have to be a Doberman or a German Shepherd. If you don't get a dog, consider leaving a dog bowl and chewed dog toy on the porch.
- Get to know your neighbors very well and understand what safety precautions are in place in the neighborhood. If there isn't a neighborhood watch program, start one.
- Look who is at the door before opening. Use a peep hole or side window to check. There are now inexpensive video cameras that hook to your computer that can be used to monitor the area outside your door. A recent check for a single camera that could be used to monitor the front door was $50 at a major discount chain.
- Use a rubber door stop to allow the door to be only partially opened a few inches so it can't suddenly be forced open. A recent check at a major hardware store indicated the price was less than $2.
- Do not let anyone know that you are or will be home alone.
- If you are alone and have to answer the door, call out in a loud voice, "Don't worry Sam/Joe/Tom, I'll get the door."
- Always lock your door or set your alarm even when just going out for mail or doing gardening in the back yard. You don't want to walk back into the house to a surprise. Lock your doors immediately after entering the house.
- Do not let any service personnel like telephone repairmen, cable company installers, gas company, furnace repairman, etc. into your home unless *you* specifically called to have them come out. Call their company to verify why they are there and what they are supposed to be doing. The BTK serial killer, Dennis Rader, gained access to a victim's home by posing as a telephone repairman. Even though she didn't think there was a problem with her telephone, one victim let him in and ten minutes later he strangled her. Never let anyone into your home unless you arranged for the repair or service.
- Have a male voice on your answering machine and/or barking dog. If you are single, have a male friend record the message.
- Use your first initial on mail box and telephone listings.
- Do not participate in telephone surveys. They have a way of getting information out of you. That's what they are trained to

do. Better simply to say, "No" and hang up.

■ Make your home look occupied by using timers on lights, TVs and radios. Have timers on lights in different rooms.

■ Make sure the exterior is well lit and bushes are cut back. Use motion detector lights by doors.

■ Lock all gates in fences.

■ Plant thorny bushes under windows and around fences. Get the thorniest bushes you can. A local nursery can make recommendations for your climate and area.

■ Cut any low limbs and remove any trellis that might allow a burglar to climb up to the second story of your home.

■ Always keep your ladders locked away in your garage.

■ Keep your garage door closed. Keep the door locked that goes from the garage into the house. Put the longer screws in the lock strike plate on this door too.

■ Walk around your house and look at it like a burglar would. How would you break in? Do you see some weaknesses in your security? Does a particular area need to be strengthened?

■ Have your house number visible or painted on the curb so that police or emergency personnel can find the address quickly.

■ Think about whether you want to have a "safe haven room" in your home. Decide if the master bedroom or one of your other rooms would be appropriate. It should have a heavy lock on the door. The door should be a solid wood or metal door. Most interior doors are hollow core doors that can easily be kicked in so have your safe room door changed to a solid core door. The room should have a portable phone, but take your cell phone into this room in case the phone lines have been cut. Consider having a weapon in this room if you are trained to use it.

■ Get a fireproof safe for your home. Place it so it is hidden or not readily visible. Keep most of your valuables in a bank safety deposit box and use your home safe for temporary storage for things you use frequently like jewelry or some emergency money.

■ Take pictures or videos of your rooms and valuables to have information for police and insurance. Make a list of serial numbers on firearms and major electronics. Keep the pictures, videos and list in your bank safety deposit box.

■ Check anyone you hire for domestic help very carefully. Ask the applicant for social security number, telephone number and address. Check their references and *actually call them* to verify the suitability of the applicant. There are also internet services that for a fee will do background checks.

- Try to vary your routine for leaving and returning.
- Have a house sitter if you are involved in a funeral, wedding, bar mitzvah etc. Criminals often read the paper and then rob houses while their occupants are attending ceremonies.
- If you put an ad in the newspaper to sell something, make sure you have a friend with you when someone arrives to look at it. Put the item on the porch or by the front door. That way you will not have to walk them through your house to look at the item.
- If you come home and your house shows signs of forced entry, **do not** go into the house. Use your cell phone or go to a neighbor to call police. Let them enter your home and check to make sure the intruder is no longer there.
- If you hear someone break in while you are at home, do not try to confront them unless you are physically threatened. Call 911 and make lots of noise to try to encourage him to leave. Intruders that are looking for cash or valuables generally do not want confrontations with the homeowner, but they may carry a weapon in case they are cornered.

Walking

- Do not wear headphones, talk on a cell phone or have other distractions that prevent your hearing or being aware of someone approaching or some car running a red light. If you do talk on a cell phone, keep looking all around and be very alert.
- You can run faster in flats or sneakers than in high heels. If you walk a lot, carry your heels and put them on when you get to your destination. You'll be more comfortable anyway!
- Keep a $20 bill in your purse or pocket. If someone confronts you and wants money, give them the $20. A smaller amount may not satisfy them. If they demand your purse or wallet, give it to them.

- Carry your purse so it is in front, the flap next to you (see Fig. 11). Place your hand on the strap to make it more difficult to grab the purse. A further precaution is to wear your purse under your coat. Wearing your purse these ways will normally dissuade the "grab and run" guy. If someone wants your purse, give it to them. Do not fight over your purse. Nothing in your purse is worth your getting hurt or perhaps worse.

Fig. 11

- Do not flash money around as you get it out or into your purse. You do not want someone to think you just emptied your bank account and it is now in your purse. Take out only the amount you need to pay for the purchase.

- Use common sense when dressing. Pay attention to the jewelry (value, amount, style) and clothing you are wearing to make sure that it conveys a message you want to send. Save that expensive jewelry for that special party or get together. When you do have to go on the street, you can use a scarf or other wrap to conceal the jewelry until you get to your destination.

- Do not take shortcuts through dark or deserted places. Stay where there are lots of people. Lots of people normally = safety. Two young girls, 14 and 16 years old, in Houston, Texas, were late getting home. Their choices were to walk 30 minutes staying on the streets or 10 minutes by walking along the railroad tracks and cutting through some woods. They choose the shortcut and crossed paths with a gang of violent young men. They were gang-raped, brutally tortured, and strangled. Even if you are late, don't take unnecessary risks to save a few minutes. By the way, the gang members were caught and are on death row or have life sentences as this book is being written, but that doesn't compensate for the loss of two young, bright lives.

- Do use a flashlight at night. It can also be used as a weapon.

- Walk opposing traffic so you can see cars coming toward you. This way someone can't pull up behind you, open a door and drag you into the car.

- Walk in the middle of the sidewalk, thus avoiding being too close to bushes or doorways.

- Walk wide around corners which will allow you to see around the corner better and give you a split second more time to react.

- If you see something on your side of the street ahead that makes you uncomfortable, either cross the street or go back the other way. It might take a little longer to go a different route, but your objective is to arrive safely at your destination.

- Whenever possible, travel with another person or persons - two is good, three better, etc.

- Use elevators, not stairs whenever possible. Stairs can be lonely places where criminals linger. If the stairs are in the open and circling upward in plain view, that's probably fine, but the closed fire escape type of stairwells should be avoided. Note - if there is a fire, you should *only* use the stairs and never elevators.

- When waiting for the elevator, stand 6 to 8 feet back from the elevator door. This prevents someone from reaching out and dragging you in, while it allows you time to evaluate whether you want to get on.

- Don't get on the elevator with anyone you don't feel comfortable with or a strange group of males.

- Stand next to the control panel on the elevator. You can push the button if you change your mind about which floor you want to get out on.

- If you feel uncomfortable or your sixth sense is tingling, get off on the next floor.

- If you want to exercise outside, go with a friend. A dog makes a great companion. If you don't have one, perhaps a neighbor will let you borrow his. Stay on main roads and populated areas. Do not go on wooded jogging trails or lonely trails near a river by yourself. At night wear reflective clothing. If you live in a dangerous area, opt to exercise indoors or go to a safer area to exercise.

- If you have to go into a questionable neighborhood, go early in the morning, never in the afternoon or evening. Turns out the bad guys tend to sleep until about noon, having been up most of the night.

- Beware of anyone requiring the help of a "Good Samaritan." We have all been brought up to help people in need, but sometimes criminals use this as a ruse. As an example, a girl was being called to by a man in the back seat of a car with the door open. He said that he was disabled and needed help closing the door. To the girl's credit, she looked around and noticed he was not parked in a handicap spot. At that moment, a male friend came along and she pointed the man out to him. The supposedly "handicapped" man jumped out of the back seat and immediately drove off. What might have happened if she had gone over to that car? Not every "Good Samaritan" situation is legitimate. Ted Bundy, the serial killer, used a cane as a ruse to elicit sympathy and get close to women. Evaluate every situation and request *very carefully*. It is perfectly fine to say, "Sorry, I can't help you, but I'll go get help," or "I'll call to get some assistance for you."
- If you go to check out a newspaper ad for some item that you want to purchase, take a friend with you. Do not go alone. If you can't get a friend, pass up the deal.
- Beware of crowds and their mood. If a crowd appears unruly, leave. Sometimes at sporting, music or other events, the crowd begins to push, and there is a real risk of being trampled. At a Who concert in Cincinnati in 1979, 11 fans died from being trampled. At a soccer match in Sheffield, England, 96 fans died after the crowd surged and pushed them against a fence separating the stands from the field. Unless you have been caught in one of these crowd situations, it is difficult to comprehend the power of a pushing crowd. You must stay upright. Immediately try to work your way to the side of the crowd and near some physical protection. If you fall down, assume the fetal position and protect your head.
- If you go to a convention or business meeting, please remove your name tag before you exit the building. It identifies you as a likely visitor to that area and allows someone to call you by name, potentially making you a more inviting target.
- Don't hitchhike – EVER! Don't EVER pick up hitchhikers!

Cars

- Have your keys out and ready to go.
- Use your radar, scanning the surroundings to see if anything appears unusual or looks amiss.
- Check to see if anyone is loitering near your car.
- Beware of a person sitting in the passenger seat of the car parked next to the driver's side of your car. As you attempt to unlock the door, he can easily get out and grab you. Although it might be a bit awkward, go around to the passenger side of your car and get in that way. Lock the doors and slide over to the driver's side.
- Beware of a van that is now parked next to you that wasn't there when you parked. A criminal can slide back the van door and grab you as you are walking up to unlock your car door. Do the same as before, get into your car on the passenger side, lock doors and slide over to the driver's side.
- As you walk towards your car, look around and glance under it.
- Look into the back seat before you get in your car. You may have to open the driver's side door to get the interior lights on, but before getting in, glance into the back seat to make sure you don't have an unwanted passenger.
- When you get into your car, *lock doors, put on seat belt, and leave* in that order. Don't make cell phone calls or make entries in your checkbook; you can do all of that later. If someone has targeted you, he is still there watching and may take advantage of your staying around. Time for you to leave.
- Always keep your gas tank at least half full. You do not want to run out of gas on a rainy night.
- Keep your car maintained and have the oil routinely checked. Make sure you have good tires, etc.
- Drive as if your life depended upon it, and it does, so no making cell phone calls, eating food, fixing makeup, etc. that would reduce your alertness. I know this is going to be a hard one, but try to minimize distractions while you are driving. Don't try to make up time if you are late, by driving faster.
- Drive defensively. Don't yell or gesture at other drivers who might have made a mistake or been rude. Smile, cut them a little slack and just assume they made a mistake. Don't get involved in a road rage scenario. If someone yells at you, smile and give them an, "Oh, I'm

so sorry" gesture. Even if it wasn't your fault this will normally defuse the situation. If you do have a problem, that's what the cell phone is for, to notify the police. Do have the local law enforcement numbers in the memory bank of your phone.

- Beware of people loitering near intersections. Keep your doors locked. Drive in the outside lane farthest from the curb without holding up traffic. Try to time the light so that you slow down, but don't stop before the light changes to green.
- When you do have to stop, stop far enough back so that you can the see the rear tires of the car in front of you. This will prevent your car being blocked in and allow you to steer around that car if necessary.
- If you drive alone at night, put on a baseball cap or other hat that gives you a male appearance.
- When you park your car try not to leave anything on the seats or clearly visible that identifies it as a female's car.
- Keep a flashlight, pen and pad in your car.
- Avoid highway rest stops that have very few people, particularly at night. Instead go to a local fast food place and buy a small drink for the use of their facilities.
- Try to let someone know where you are going and when you expect to return. If something does happen and you are overdue, someone can take steps to begin to locate you or alert the appropriate individuals.
- If you feel your car has been deliberately bumped, put on your flashers and drive to the nearest public place like a gas station to inspect damage.
- If you think you are being followed, turn four or five corners. If the car is still behind you, *do not drive to your home*, drive to the nearest police station or well lit public place like a gas station. You can blow your horn to attract attention if necessary, using the recognized Morse code signal for an emergency which is SOS; three short honks followed by three long honks followed by three short honks. Keep repeating this sequence.
- If you get a flat tire, drive slowly to the nearest gas station. You may ruin the tire and rim, but it is a safer course of action. If you are out in the middle of nowhere, you may want to carry an inflation canister that inflates the tire and puts in a sealant. The local hardware or automotive stores have these canisters.

- If you have a car problem, pull well off the road and use your cell phone to call for assistance. If someone approaches, roll your window down 1 inch and say, "Thank you, but the police have already been called." If they claim they are the police, thank them and ask them to call a uniformed patrol unit. A legitimate law enforcement official should always be willing to comply with your request. A fold up windshield sunscreen that says "Call Police" can be helpful. If you are on a desolate road, you may want to put on warm clothes, get out of the car, and hide in bushes away from the car. You may become a target if you remain in the car. If a police car stops you can come out. If any other car comes you will have to assess the situation.
- If an unmarked car flashes its lights at you or has the alternating flashing headlights the police sometimes use, be cautious. Put on your hazard flashers and drive slowly to the nearest gas station or public place. Call the police on your cell phone and tell them what is happening and that you are driving to the nearest gas station. If a plain clothes person approaches you flashing a badge, ask for a uniformed officer to be called.
- Back into the parking spot whenever you can. You have to back up when you leave, so why not as you are parking. This way you can make a quicker exit.
- Do not pull into a space next to a car occupied with men.
- Use the parking valet service at restaurants and hotels. It is going to cost you a few dollars, but you are not going to have to go into a dark garage or park down a questionable street. Do have a separate valet key that you can give them. *Do not* give them the car keys with your house keys. They might make a copy of your house keys while you are gone, and they have your license plate number.
- If there is no valet service, park as closely as you can to the entrance, where it is well lit, and not next to bushes.
- Consider getting an OnStar type service which allows you to contact help anytime you are in your car. Other car security items are LoJack, 800-535-6522, which can locate a stolen car and The Club, 800-527-3345, which locks the steering wheel.
- Never get out and leave the car running, no matter how quick the trip will be into the store or because you want to keep the AC going since it is hot outside.

- *Never ever leave your children in the car* no matter what their age. On several occasions I have seen women dash into stores, leaving the car running, doors unlocked and with what appeared to be young girls, 10 to 12 years old, sitting in the passenger seat. What were they thinking? There have been tragic cases where babies have gotten overheated after being left in cars while the mother dashed in to do some quick shopping. Never ever leave your children in the car alone.

- Place valuables or purchases in your trunk or cover them with a blanket before leaving your home or office, reducing the potential of you or your car being targeted. If you are going into a gym, take your purse with you and place it in a gym locker rather than leaving it your car. It takes thieves less than a minute to smash a window and grab your purse. Thieves target gym parking lots knowing a lot of women do not take their purses into the gym.

- In parking lots, walk through the wide main aisles. It may be necessary to walk a little extra, but do not cut between the parked cars.

- If someone displays a weapon and demands your car, get out on the passenger side if you can, and throw the keys towards them, but not too close, and run.

- If someone grabs you while you are getting into the car throw the keys away so he can't abduct you and take you to crime scene #2.

- If someone gets in the car, immediately get out and run. Do not hesitate; seconds count here.

- If there are children in the car, lean over the front seat, get them and then get out - then throw the keys. If you get out and then try to get the children out, the criminal might take your keys, get in the car and drive off with your children.

- Never give a ride to a stranger or a friend of friend of a friend.

- Don't drive if you have had anything that impairs your driving – alcohol, medication, etc.

- Don't drive in the rain with your cruise control on. If your tires lose contact with the road because of the wetness, the cruise control will cause you to accelerate, perhaps losing control of the vehicle.

- If your car won't start, look around to see if anyone is standing nearby. If so, keep the doors locked and use your cell phone. If no one is around, immediately go back to the place you just left and make your phone call for assistance. If it is at night, you may want to call a taxi and deal with the stalled car in the daylight.

Public Transportation

- Trying not to arrive very early for your bus prevents having to wait too long standing on the street. If you do have to wait, try to wait in a nearby store and not on the street. Be alert, looking all around you periodically.
- Sit closer to the driver. Do not sit near the exit door since someone could grab your purse or packages on the way out. Sit in an aisle seat so you can move more easily if there is a problem with your seat companion.
- On a subway car, try to aim for one of the corners that you can place your belongings against.
- Do not set your packages on the seat beside or under you; instead keep them in your lap. You won't forget them, and they are harder for others to grab.
- Do not get into an empty subway car. Try to get in a car that has women in it already or with other women who are getting ready to board that car. Make sure the car is well lit.
- Do not stand at an isolated section of a platform. Stay near people unless they are a problem.
- Don't use your laptop in the subway or otherwise display anything of value.
- Do not fall asleep. If you do, you may wake up to find all of your possessions are missing.
- Do not stay in a car that has someone who is drunk or otherwise acting strangely. Get off at the next stop and get onto a different car.
- Look outside the car before you get off. If there is a group of unruly men, you may want to get off at the next stop.
- Get out first or with the group exiting. Do not be a straggler. Remember in nature, stragglers are vulnerable.

Shopping

- Take only those credit cards and cash that you need. Most people carry around far more credit cards than they need. Don't carry your social security card with you. Memorize the number.

- Shop with a friend, or even better, friends.
- Holiday shopping is notorious for higher levels of criminal activity. Take extra precautions and be more alert during these times.
- As you walk into the store, look around to see if the employees are acting normally. If they are all standing still and appear to be looking at one or more individuals, you may have walked in on a robbery in progress or other problem. Leave immediately.
- If you see someone looking around furtively to see if anyone or security cameras are watching them, they may be a shoplifter or preparing for a robbery.
- Keep your purse on you, not in the shopping cart or on the floor while you are deciding on your next purchase. You not only run the risk of losing money, but more importantly, someone might use the documents in your purse to steal your identity. You have been to grocery stores and routinely seen unattended carts with purses while the owners are further down the aisle. It only takes a second for a purse to disappear when it is left unattended.
- Don't allow yourself to be distracted. Ruses can be spilling something on you, dropping packages, bumping into you, etc. Be immediately alert since all of these may be deliberate attempts to steal your purse, your purchases or pick your pockets.
- When paying in cash take out the minimum amount to pay the bill. Do not take out a large amount of money and then return it to your purse. Someone may have been watching and now identified your purse as a lucrative target.
- Be aware of the color clothing that you pick for yourself or children. It is unfortunate, but true, that in particular areas some colors have gang connotations and can bring unwanted attention.
- Be careful when going to changing rooms or restrooms. Do not put your purse on the floor where someone can grab it and run. Place it on a shelf, the top of the toilet tank or your lap.
- Go to restrooms in the store rather than to the mall restroom which typically is down a long lonely corridor in an out of the way place.
- If you see someone lounging outside the store door, wait until another shopper starts to leave and go out with them. Even if you don't know that shopper, the fact that now there are two or more of you reduces the risk of you being accosted.

- Use your radar to scan the sidewalk and parking lot as you go to your car.
- Try to have only one arm full of packages when you go to your car. This leaves your other hand free in order to have your keys out and potentially respond to an assailant.
- If you bring packages out to your car before finishing shopping, get in and move your car to a new location. If someone is watching you they will think you are leaving rather than waiting to ambush you the next time you come out if you didn't move your car.
- Use grocery store bag boys to escort you out to your car, especially at night even if you only have a couple of sacks. The stores provide this as a service and the bag boys are invariably very courteous. Take advantage of this. Should you choose to go alone to your vehicle and something seems strange, out of place, or someone loitering nearby, come back to request an escort by a bag boy or security personnel.
- Watch your credit card being scanned and make sure you get it back along with the copy of the receipt. If it is out of your sight, like at a restaurant, make sure it is your card when you get it back.
- When you leave a restaurant and plan to take a cab, have the restaurant call a cab so you don't have to stand out on the street trying to flag down a cab.

Bank/ATM

- Try to use banks instead of ATMs. If you have to use an ATM, look around carefully to see if anyone is loitering nearby. Use the ATM at the bank or inside a commercial business. Do not use one that is isolated.
- If you must use ATMs, go in the daytime, looking carefully to see if anyone is loitering nearby. If you have to get money at night, use an ATM inside a grocery store or other busy place of business, being alert to anyone who appears to be watching you.
- Wait until the person leaves before you approach the ATM. Stand sideways in front of the ATM while still blocking the view of the screen so that you can see around you and particularly if someone is coming up behind you. Remember to take your ATM card when you are finished.

- As you walk into the bank, check to see if the employees are behaving normally. If not, get out immediately since there may be a robbery in progress.
- Conduct your financial affairs inside the bank. Count your money and put it away inside the bank. Don't walk outside holding the envelope with cash, or worse, thumbing through the bills making sure it is the right amount.
- Use your radar, scanning from side to side and all around as you leave the bank.
- Get in your car, lock the doors and leave. Do not make entries in your check book or linger longer than absolutely necessary.

Office/business

- Make sure visitor access is limited and strangers cannot wander through office areas.
- Visible security cameras are a good deterrent.
- Make sure all outside doors are locked after hours.
- Do not let anyone know that you will be the one to close the business at night. Try to have more than one person there when the business is closed up for the day.
- Try not to work late by yourself. Try to arrange a schedule so that two of you work and leave at the same time. If you are scheduled to work late, take a cooler with food in it to avoid going to vending machines in isolated areas.
- Leave in a group whenever possible.
- Ask security guards to escort you to your car at night.
- Be very careful on any job that requires being alone with a strange male. Real estate agents should carefully vet a client before showing him vacant houses. They should get his address, phone number, and copy of his driver's license. They should tell their manager or assistant where they going, which properties are being shown and what time they plan to return. The real estate agent is an example, but the principles apply to other jobs with variations based on the specifics of the job.
- If you take funds to the bank, do not use a bank bag. Use some other bag that does not look as if it contains money. Try to have two people go together to make deposits.
- Lock your purse in a desk drawer or file cabinet during the day,

no matter how safe your workplace.

- Be careful of restrooms that the public can access. Do not consider restrooms safe havens since an assailant could follow you in.
- If a co-worker displays a marked change in personality or hostility to other co-workers, bring it to the attention of your supervisor or the Human Relations department on a confidential basis.
- Document and report any sexual harassment to your employer's human relations department. Companies have strong policies against sexual harassment since they can be liable and major judgments have been brought against companies. If your employer does not take action you can go to the Employee Equal Opportunity Commission, EEOC, under Title VII of the Civil Rights Act. Reporting incidents of harassment should put an end to the problem and prevent further escalation.

Relationships

- Avoid associating with anyone that has criminal behavior. Your personal safety is compromised by being around individuals that are involved in drugs or other illegal activities. Crime and violence go hand in hand. While you may not be doing anything illegal, if you are around criminal activities, you may suffer violence and personal injury. Don't risk it. Find new friends – your life may depend upon it.
- Do not tolerate abuse or stay in any relationship that is abusive. Your personal safety may be at risk in an abusive relationship. See later chapters on Children/Teenagers and Domestic Violence.

Let's review **Avoidance**:

- ✓ Prevention is about avoiding problems.
- ✓ Mark those ideas you should be doing and implement those ideas as part of your safety plan.
- ✓ Most of the avoidance ideas are common sense – use good judgment.
- ✓ Check your residence to see if its security can be improved.

- ✓ Your cell phone is the single most important safety item.
- ✓ Don't try to save time by taking risky shortcuts or driving faster.
- ✓ Walking, shopping or traveling with one or more friends is generally safer.
- ✓ Conduct financial transactions during the day inside the bank.
- ✓ Don't associate with anyone involved in criminal activities.
- ✓ Periodically review your progress and how well you have done in making the **Avoidance** suggestions routine.

Chapter 4

Action

"Self defense is the use of force to protect oneself or one's family from harm; self defense is generally justified if it is proportional to the danger posed." – Legal Definitions

Y ou may have done everything right, but you still may find yourself at the wrong place at the wrong time and have to defend yourself or family. This is not unlike driving down the highway when a car suddenly careens across the road, running into you. Things happen. When they do, you need to be prepared. You have a fundamental right to defend yourself against an attacker. The fourth A is about having to take **Action** against an attacker.

There are various types of confrontations. These range from someone verbally abusing you to someone potentially trying to cause you great bodily harm. You will learn to use various tools to deal with these situations. We are going to begin with **Verbal Self-Defense.**

The first situations we want to deal with are those where you are approached, but not physically touched or significantly threatened. Let's start with a scenario where someone approaches you in a bar, the grocery store or wherever and wants something – a date, to buy you a beer or cup of coffee, wants you to go home with him, etc. Assuming you are not interested, tell him politely "No thank you." If he stays and persists, you can tell him less politely "No thank you" and/or go directly to the steps for **Verbal Self-Defense** outlined below.

The second scenario is the angry person. You may have seen this happen in traffic accident altercations or some other incident. The typical, but not always, warning signs of an impending confrontation of this type are a red face, clenched fists, arms waving, raised voice and movement towards you. Follow the **Verbal Self-Defense** steps to handle this situation.

In a third scenario you may be approached by someone in a non-threatening manner and that asks you the time, or other seemingly innocent question. Be aware that criminals sometimes come up to "interview" their potential victims to see how they might react or perhaps assess their ability to fight back. If you are approached, just keep moving, and remember it is fine to say, "Sorry, I'm in a hurry," etc., *as long as you keep moving*. Move quickly to put distance between you and the interviewer and if possible, move to a safe position, such as a place of business, with a group of other people, or inside your *locked* car. If he continues to follow you and you cannot get to a place of safety, turn and face the person and follow the steps for **Verbal Self-Defense** outlined below.

In a fourth scenario a person may deliberately brush up against you or grab you inappropriately. He may be testing you to determine whether you have weak or strong boundaries. If you are close to a place of safety, such as a place of business, you may decide to go there quickly. Otherwise turn to him immediately, taking a strong stance and say, "Leave me alone!" or "Go away!" Show them you have strong boundaries and will not tolerate anything inappropriate. He also learns you are prepared to defend yourself which is a strong prevention message. If he doesn't immediately leave or back off, follow the steps for **Verbal Self-Defense** below.

Verbal Self-Defense

- Show no fear and remain calm.
- Take a strong stance with one foot in front, knee bent, leaning slightly forward (hopefully you have already assumed this posture as part of **Attitude** training). Position yourself *two steps* away and slightly to the side. This distance prevents the person from suddenly stepping forward and grabbing you. Increase the distance if he is a tall person with longer legs
- Remain objective and listen to what he is saying; maybe there is a simple misunderstanding. If so, you have an opportunity to get

that cleared up. It is perfectly correct to say, "My mistake - sorry," even if it wasn't your fault. Saying that doesn't cost you anything. It could be a simple solution to solving the problem. Don't ever let ego or pride get involved making you defend something.

- Communicate calmly and clearly. Do not antagonize the person by calling him names or questioning his IQ level. You want to resolve the issue without harm to either party.
- You may want to de-escalate by being assertive, but without challenging the individual. Different comments may be used to de-escalate the situation such as, "Calm down so we can discuss the problem," "You have a point, let's talk about this," etc. You get the idea. You want to calm the situation so that the problem can be discussed and resolved.

- If the individual continues to be threatening, you should extend your arms out with palms facing him, and state strongly, "Back Off" (see Fig. 12). This is an assertive posture, not an aggressive one. You may have to repeat the "Back Off" several times for the message to finally get through.

Fig. 12

- I do not advocate saying, "Back off or <u>I'll hurt you</u>." This can sound like a challenge which may provoke him to prove you can't really hurt him. There are other times when a strong verbal threat may be effective in making your assailant reconsider his actions. You have to decide based on your assessment of the situation.
- At this point, don't justify your actions or answer any questions. It is time for him to back off and leave. If he doesn't back off, you may be forced to use physical techniques described below.

39

Physical Self-Defense

If the unwanted person continues to advance or appears to be threatening from the start, action may be necessary. The **Fight** or **Flight** decision must be made before you are within his grabbing distance. If **Flight** is an option and you can *successfully escape*, do it. Don't hesitate; just bolt, running as fast as you can. Reacting quickly will likely catch the person off guard and give you an advantage. **Flight,** if it is an option, is the better alternative since the likelihood of suffering physical harm is much lower. Never forget that your goal is to escape. If there is any doubt about **Flight** or being able to escape, face your attacker and be prepared to defend yourself. If you have to fight, accept the fact that you will likely suffer some injury. This acceptance will get you past the concern or paralyzing fear, "Oh, but I might get hurt." Accept the fact that you might get hurt, BUT you intend to survive, and inflict greater pain on your assailant.

When you are confronted or threatened, you need to make a split second decision on how to respond. *There is no standard answer on what to do. You will need to assess the situation and make your own best judgment on how to proceed.* You will need to decide quickly what to do by assessing the situation and making your best judgment. How far away is safety? If you run, can you make it? Will someone respond quickly to shouts for help? How far away is help? Does he want just the cash or jewelry or does he want you? How big/strong does the person appear? Does he have a weapon? Do you think you can verbally persuade him to stop? Is there more than one person confronting you? Are you by yourself or do you have children with you? What level of self-defense skills do you have? This is a partial list of all the questions that your brain will process in milliseconds to help you make a decision on how to respond and what level of force to use. You only have a moment to react, so act instantly once you make your decision. Again, the decision is **Flight** or **Fight**. If **Flight** is an option and you can successfully escape, then that is the better alternative. *Don't hesitate; just bolt. Run like crazy to the nearest place of safety.*

If **Flight** is not an option and the person physically threatening you wants your cash, jewelry, or car, give it to them. Keep the money in front of you where they can focus on it and less on you. Throw the money toward them, but not directly to them, so they have to retrieve it; giving you a chance to escape. All of those material things can be replaced; you can not. Let me repeat this: don't hesitate; give them the cash and run, screaming. You are too important to let anything happen to you. There are still things in life you need to do other than dying for the contents of your purse. The attacker has to decide – the cash or chase the screaming woman.

Now, you have tried all options to avoid physical conflict, but at some point you may be grabbed or need to physically defend yourself or your family from harm. If you decide to take action, you must commit 110% to that effort, go for broke, or as poker players say, "All in." You must commit all the strength and ferocity that you can muster. You must be your attacker's worst nightmare. You must give it your best and maximum effort, for this may be a life and death situation for you. When your life is at stake you must be prepared to inflict serious injury on your assailant in order to incapacitate him and allow you to escape.

Generally, attackers desire easy targets that they can deal with quickly and quietly. They don't want a fight where they might get hurt or a protracted, noisy fight in the middle of a mall parking lot that will attract bystanders or the police. While criminals are normally looking for easy targets, they will take on difficult targets if that is their specific objective or person of interest. So while a burglar might normally skip a house that has a guard dog, if he thinks that house has lots of money or other valuables, he will deal with the dog and try to burglarize the house.

In most cases if you inflict enough pain on an attacker, he will quit. Therefore the more pain the attacker suffers, the quicker he stops. You should be aware that a criminal on drugs or pain killers may not respond to pain at all. In those situations joint locks or kicks to the knee, causing him to lose his balance, may be more effective. Sometimes just the length of a fight will cause the attacker to give up and run. In an ideal case, you would be able to disable or dissuade an attacker quickly by using a self-defense technique, but if not, the longer the fight continues the more it is likely to attract attention and bring the aid of others.

A recent example of what a strong defense can do was demonstrated in Houston, Texas when a man attempted to abduct a 14 year old girl and her 8 year old brother. The girl fought vigorously, kicking and hitting, and yelled for her brother to run for help. The girl continued to fight and the man released her and fled. Criminals want easy targets and aren't expecting someone to put up a vigorous defense. Moral to the story; size isn't the issue, heart is.

Let's take a look at the weapons you are carrying. When I ask this question in my classes, the students immediately look in their purses, pulling out pens, pepper spray and keys. These can be effective defense weapons, but not if they are in *the bottom of your purse*. The bad guy is *not* going to wait around while you search for your weapons.

Let me share some thoughts regarding commonly purchased weapons. Pepper spray's active ingredient is oleoresin capsicum which is the highly irritating ingredient in red pepper that burns the tongue. The heat is measured in Scoville units. A Bell pepper has about 5,000 Scoville units while a Habanero pepper has about 2 million. The higher the percent capsicum, the more effective it is. Something in the 5 to 10% range is good with Scoville units of at least 100,000. It causes involuntary closure of the eyelids, constricts the breathing passages and hurts likes the dickens. Pepper spray comes in all sizes of containers to fit on a key chain, in your purse or on your belt. It also comes in large cans like spray paint and is used as a hiker's defense against grizzly bears. That alone should speak to the effectiveness of pepper spray. In fact, when my wife and I backpacked in Alaska's Denali National Park, we carried it all the time on our belts where we could have accessed it in an instant had it been necessary.

For pepper spray to be effective, these precautions need to be followed. Have it out in your hand or readily accessible, avoid spraying it into the wind or it will blow back, incapacitating you while potentially helping your attacker, and keep pepper spray new and not out of date. The spray should be directed towards the mucous membranes; the eyes and nostrils. A stream spray will give you better distance, but it requires a bit more accuracy than a cone spray dispersal system. Don't spray it in a car or small area or it will affect everyone equally. It cannot be carried on airplanes.

Other weapons such as Taser guns, with their wired darts that deliver an electrical charge, can be very effective, but they have to be available and you have to know how use them. Heavy clothing and leather jackets may impede the darts. They are not small to carry around, and you must be able to deploy them instantly. Stun guns use a charge of electricity to incapacitate an attacker, but they require actually touching the assailant for up to seven seconds to be effective. The bad guy is not going to stand still while you are doing this. You may choose to carry a Kubotan, which is a plastic or metal cylinder about 5 ½ inches long. This can be used for striking and poking. It typically is attached to your key chain. If you carry one, get training on how to use it and keep it accessible.

If you are in a "Right to Carry" state and choose to carry a firearm, you must be licensed, trained and be mentally prepared to use lethal force. Even if you are properly licensed there will be many places - i.e. airports, courthouses and other government buildings, establishments that serve alcohol - where you will likely not be able to legally carry your firearm. The National Rifle Association (NRA) offers very good firearms training, hosting various classes throughout the country. I stress the training because you must access the weapon quickly and be able to hit your intended target. Even police officers find hitting a target at close range under stressful conditions difficult. They also understand that, if the criminal is less than 21 feet away and charging towards them, they will probably be unable to draw their firearm before the criminal reaches them. This is really important. If your attacker is less than 21 feet away, you will most likely have to use a physical self-defense technique unless you have your gun in your hand. You simply will not have time to draw it. Be aware that even if you are properly licensed, you will most likely be required by the laws of your jurisdiction to conceal your weapon, thus reducing its accessibility. If you have some warning, such as hearing noises in your home, or some other indication of trouble, the firearm can be a highly effective self-defense weapon. You do need to take bystanders into consideration and must thoroughly understand the laws regarding the use of a firearm, or you may be the one going to jail. There are other serious risks and responsibilities associated with having a gun in the house and around children. All of these factors need to be carefully weighed.

In all cases, if you select a weapon, it must be readily accessible. If a weapon is not quickly available to deploy, it might as well be a paperweight.

There are many items that can be used as improvised weapons in the home in an emergency. Hair spray, oven cleaner, pointed brushes, kitchen knives, scissors, pencils, canes, umbrellas, flashlights and many other typical household items can be used against an intruder. Almost anything you can grab can be used as a club or weapon in a real emergency.

I happen to like the weapons you have with you even when you're taking a shower. They are always with you and readily accessible! Let's identify those weapons starting from the top of the head down:

- Forehead – can be used against attacker's face.
- Back of head - can be used against attackers face if they grab you from behind.
- Teeth – self explanatory.
- Shoulders – can be used against attacker's body.
- Back – when grabbed from behind, the back can be arched slightly and slammed into the chest of the attacker.
- Elbows – they can be used for a variety of strikes and are extremely strong. They can cause a devastating blow.
- Hands – all parts of the hand can used for striking; the knuckles, the edge of the hand (little finger side), the ridge side by the index finger, and the palm.
- Fingers – these can be used for grabbing, poking, and striking.
- Hips – if you are grabbed from behind, thrust your hips or rump sharply into your attacker's stomach.
- Knees – very effective for striking, particularly the groin.
- Feet – martial artists will tell you how effective feet can be. Legs are longer and more powerful than arms and therefore deliver greater power. The top of the foot, the sides of the foot and the bottom of the foot can all be used to deliver devastating blows.

Almost all parts of the body can be used as weapons. It is simply a matter of learning effective use of these natural weapons you have readily available. They are with you at all times and you cannot leave them behind. They are also legal to carry in all states.

We have identified the basic weapons with us at all times. Now let's understand the vulnerable points of an attacker. There are around 700 pressure points on the body. Martial artists focus on approximately 120 points as they deliver their strikes and kicks. It should be noted that about 36 of these points are potentially lethal when struck with enough force.

The **target areas** on an attacker's body are:

- Temple
- Eyes
- Nose
- Ears
- Side of neck
- Throat
- Solar Plexus

- Arms
- Hands
- Fingers
- Ribs
- Groin
- Knees
- Feet

This list does not cover every potential point on a body, but it does tell you there are numerous targets on which to execute self-defense techniques. It does take training to understand how to deliver an effective strike or kick to the selected target. This leads to a discussion of the most appropriate strikes and kicks that a woman can execute effectively with minimal training. If you take martial arts training for a number of years, you will be able to demonstrate a high level of understanding of self-defense techniques. This book does not intend to try to make you a black belt, nor does it claim to be a comprehensive book of self-defense techniques. Rather it selects a few techniques that women can easily learn to use in an emergency. These techniques have been carefully selected for their ease to execute while delivering maximum impact. It is better to learn a few techniques well than know a hundred that you are unable to execute properly. While a variety of attacks will be discussed, you will see that the same defense techniques get used in various combinations to deal with those attacks.

You will learn a variety of techniques to use as responses to physical confrontations, including everything from simple disengagement techniques to potentially lethal strikes. The strikes and kicks discussed below can cause significant damage, including death. You should use the appropriate response and a reasonable level of force to deal with any attacker. In all cases, once the assailant is incapacitated or ceases any further attempt to assault you, you should withhold any additional strikes or kicks, since the law most likely will view inflicting damage beyond this point as unjustified.

As a general rule, you can respond with an equal or slightly greater force than your assailant. The law typically requires that you use reasonable force in response to a threat. Remember law enforcement will likely be looking at the incident after the fact to determine what went on, who did what, and was your response appropriate. (Further general information on self-defense guidelines is available on pages 167-169). State and local laws do vary and I urge to be familiar with them.

You will have to decide which techniques to use and the level of force that is reasonable and appropriate to the threat. You normally do not have the right to use force against someone verbally harassing you. If a man grabs your wrist in a bar making you uncomfortable, but is not threatening you, you would be justified in using only the degree of force immediately necessary to remove the unwanted touch, such as one of the simple release techniques taught below. As the threat escalates, you have the right to increase your level of force in responding. If you are being slapped, a kick or a non-lethal strike would be more appropriate than responding with a lethal technique. If a man grabs you in the parking lot and tries to drag you to his car, you have every reason to believe he is threatening serious physical harm and possibly threatening your life. In that case, you would want to respond in a very forceful manner to get away and not be put into the car. If a man tells you he is going to kill you right now, you would want to have a very forceful response doing everything necessary to prevent that from happening.

Now the questions come up. What should I do in different situations? How much force should I use? These are very good questions.

So how do you decide how much force to use? That is a judgment call that must be made by you based on your best assessment of the threat situation. Every situation is going to be different so there is no standard answer. What demand or threat is he making? How serious do you believe the threat to be? What is his body language? Is there more than one person or a weapon? If he just wants your purse, give it to him. On the other hand if he is threatening to hurt you or your children, then a higher force level response would be appropriate. If you are being attacked, you must make the decision instantly and respond with your best judgment of the appropriate force. Because of the extreme pressure under which you would be required to make a decision, it greatly behooves you to think through potential scenarios beforehand.

To help you develop a methodology to analyze what would constitute an appropriate response, I have divided the types of self-defense techniques into three levels of increasingly stronger responses.

Level I	Simple disengagements and releases generally causing no or minor pain.
Level II	Techniques that will cause pain and possibly injury.
Level III	Techniques that will cause pain, injury and in some cases may cause death if applied with enough force.

These general categories are designed to allow you to select the response that you believe is appropriate for the situation. You should understand that a violently applied Level I response may be elevated to a Level II and in the same manner a Level II might become a Level III. On the other hand, a weakly applied Level III might become a Level II or even a Level I. To be effective, the techniques we're going to discuss do need to be applied with force and determination. Do not be timid about applying these techniques.

When the assailant is no longer a threat, you should make an immediate escape. Make your escape as soon as possible. Do be careful about stopping too early only to have the criminal continue his attack. Make sure there is *no continuing threat* before ceasing your actions. Even when you stop, do not let your guard down until you have reached safety or help has arrived. I do urge you to check federal, state and your local laws regarding self-defense.

Never try to meet force with force, since he will more likely be bigger and stronger than you. It is far better to slip to the side, avoiding the direct attack, and then quickly respond with a kick or strike. Always try to get out of the way of someone charging or trying to punch you. Slide to the side or duck out of the way at the last moment so that he charges by or his punch misses. I say at the last moment because if you move before he commits to his attack, he will just change the direction of his charge or punch. Once he has committed to his attack, it is harder for him to change the direction of it, thus allowing you to avoid it and counter. Again, if you can escape before he charges or tries to punch you, do that!

Let's begin by learning how to apply the lowest or minimum level of response to a threat.

Level I

We're going to start by looking at how to deal with someone grabbing your wrist and how to escape this grasp.

Wrist Release

This is a good technique to achieve a release from a grasp. The thumb is the weakest part of the grip and you ALWAYS want to work against this point. If your wrist is grabbed, quickly rotate your arm and hand in a circle around his arm, going over the thumb towards the back of his hand. This will work against the thumb of his grip and free your arm. As an example, if your right wrist is grabbed by his left hand, you would execute a clockwise circle. If your left wrist was grabbed by his right hand you would execute a counterclockwise circle to the outside of his body (see Fig. 13-16).

Fig. 13 Grabbed by same side hand

Fig. 14 Roll hand over top

Fig. 15 Continue roll   Fig. 16 Complete the release

When the right wrist is grabbed by the right hand it is called a cross hand grab and the same technique is used working against the thumb (see Fig. 17-20). Circle your hand counterclockwise (to the outside of his body), going over the thumb and continuing around to affect the release.

Fig. 17 Grabbed – cross hand   Fig. 18 Roll hand over top

| Fig. 19 Continue around | Fig. 20 Hand freed |

The escape from a wrist grasp cannot be done slowly. As soon as your attacker feels your hand begin to move he will tighten down. It is therefore very important to do these moves quickly. Do not hesitate. A strong man might try to stop you from making the circle move. No problem, when he stops your circle move by gripping stronger, reverse the circle and go the other way. He will resist that move and try to stop your circle that way. Quickly reverse direction and circle back in the original direction. This will free you from his grasp.

The wrist release is easier to see if you have a partner practice with you. Practice until you can execute the circle move without hesitation. You can further distract the attacker by stomping his toes or poking towards his eyes. Remember, the brain can handle only so many inputs at one time. If it is dealing with stomped toes, it is not thinking as strongly about preventing your escape from the grasp. This release works very well. It should be taught to your children to allow them to escape anyone trying to grab them.

The escaping grasps techniques are really best practiced with a partner. Get with a friend and practice these so that they become second nature when anyone grabs you. This can be practiced with no harm to either partner.

Wrist Lock Turn

The wrist lock turn is an extremely effective technique and can defeat a number of different grasps. This is a very powerful joint lock and is a basic aikido technique called kotegaeshi. This is a versatile defense move that can be used in many situations and needs to be practiced with a partner until you become adept at it.

It starts by grasping the back of your attacker's hand, placing your thumb towards the little finger knuckle (see Fig. 21-24). If your attacker has a large hand, extend your thumb as far across the back of his hand as you can. Your thumb should be on the back of his hand, with your other four fingers grasping the base of his thumb and your fingertips extending into his palm over the base of his thumb. Your little finger should start at the wrist and the other three should be extending up to the meat of the thumb. To execute the wrist turn, push your thumb toward your finger tips with a rotating motion. This creates a twisting motion of his hand causing instant pain in his wrist. Take your second hand and place it on your thumb to help with the twisting motion and to apply more pressure. Continue twisting the hand while forcing it toward your attacker's elbow. Turn his hand towards the outside of his body. His right hand would be turned counterclockwise and his left would be turned clockwise. As you continue to twist the wrist, your assailant will be forced to the ground to save his wrist from being broken. If the wrist turn is done quickly, and with enough force, it will break the wrist. This technique is best learned by training with a partner.

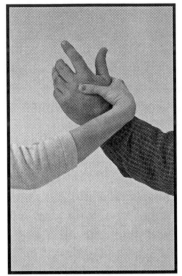

Fig. 21 Thumb on back

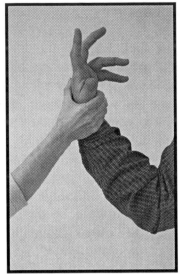

Fig. 22 Begin turning

Note the finger placement carefully; thumb on the back of this large hand and the four fingers grabbing around the thumb into palm.

Fig. 23 2nd hand assists

Fig. 24 Continue turning

Use your second hand to add power to the turn. Go slowly when practicing with a partner. This is a very powerful wrist lock and quickly causes pain. Have your partner tap their thigh or chest with their hand to indicate their pain limit has been reached. Immediately release them.

We examined the left hand being turned; now let's look at the right hand being turned (see Fig. 25-27).

Fig. 25 Thumb on back   Fig. 26 Use second hand

Fig. 27 Continue turning

Let's examine a couple of ways the wrist lock turn might be employed. We used a **wrist release** to escape a wrist grab before. Now we can use the **wrist lock turn**. If your attacker grabs your left wrist with his left hand (cross hand grab), place your right hand on the back of his with your thumb on his little finger knuckle (your palm across the back of his hand), and your four fingers grabbing the fleshy part of his thumb. Instantly upon applying pressure to his hand, yank your grasped hand free by pulling the wrist through the point where his thumb and index finger come together. Your four fingers pulling on his thumb will help open his grip so you can free your wrist. Immediately bring your freed hand up on the top of his hand to help apply additional turning pressure. Strongly twist your attacker's hand clockwise which will take him to the ground (see Fig. 28-32). Run to safety.

Fig. 28 Grabbed – cross hand   Fig. 29 Grab attacker's hand
and begin to turn

The placement of the fingers in Fig. 29 is shown in more detail in Fig. 29A.

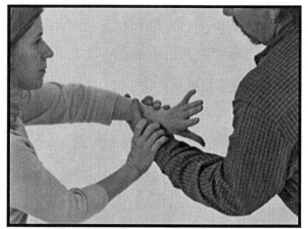

Fig. 29A

Fig. 30 Pull held hand free

Fig. 30A Detail of freeing held hand

Free the grabbed hand (Fig. 30A) by pulling your wrist through where the attacker's thumb and index finger come together. Use the freed hand to apply additional pressure to turn the attacker's hand (Fig. 31-32).

Fig. 31 2nd hands assists turn   Fig. 32 Continue turning hand

In the very same manner, if he grabs your right wrist with his right hand, execute a wrist lock turn, only this time you would turn the hand counterclockwise. You always turn/twist the hand to the outside of his body. His right hand would always get turned counterclockwise and his left hand clockwise.

Reverse Wrist Turn

If he grabs your right hand with his left hand (same side hand grab), turn your right hand so the palm is facing up. Reach underneath his hand, with your free hand keeping this palm up also. Grab the fleshy part of his thumb with your four fingers and place your thumb on the little finger knuckle while your palm covers the back of his hand. Yank your grasped hand towards your right shoulder while using the other hand to twist his hand clockwise. Immediately bring the freed hand back to help finish the wrist turn, taking your attacker to the ground (see Fig. 33-37).

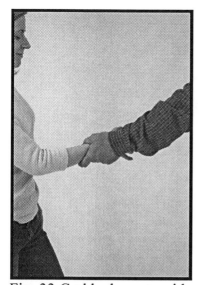

Fig. 33 Grabbed – same side

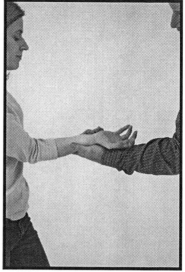

Fig. 34 Turn palm up

Fig. 35 Grab underneath

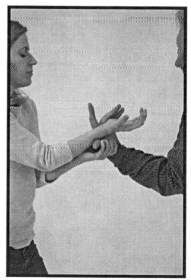

Fig. 36 Free hand & begin turn

Look carefully at the hand positions and how the fingers are used to peel off the attacker's thumb. Your thumb needs to be on the back of the attacker's hand towards his little finger knuckle to provide the leverage necessary to begin turning the hand.

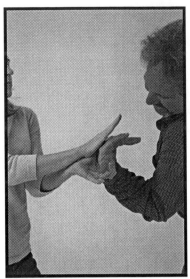

Fig. 37 Use hand to assist turn

Finish this technique by continuing to turn his hand far enough to force him to the ground. He will have to go to the ground to prevent his wrist from being broken. Escape immediately to safety.

A similar action can be done if your left hand is grabbed by his right. Turn your left hand up so you can see the palm. Reach underneath with your right hand to grab his hand, yank your left hand to your left shoulder and use it to apply additional pressure to complete the wrist turn this time turning his hand counterclockwise. Turn his hand strongly to force him to the ground.

Both Wrists Grabbed From Front

Use the **reverse wrist turn** technique as you just practiced for the same side hand grab. Cross your hands in front of you with the palms up. Use the lower hand to reach under your attacker's hand; grabbing his hand and executing a reverse wrist turn (see Fig. 38-41).

Fig 38 Both wrists grabbed   Fig. 39 Reach under & grab

Fig. 39A Detail of reaching under

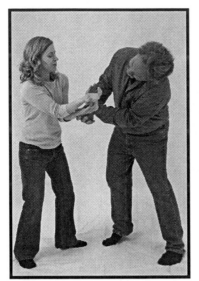
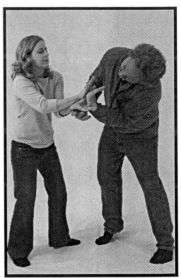

Fig. 40 Free upper hand   Fig. 41 Use to assist twist

Both Wrists Grabbed From Back

Bring your hands together behind your back so that one hand can grab the attacker's hand holding your other wrist (second hand). Grab the hand so that your thumb is on the back of his hand and execute a wrist turn. Peel the attacker's thumb away from your wrist and jerk your second hand free.

Fig. 42 Grabbed   Fig. 43 Apply wrist turn

Turn to face him and immediately use your freed hand to assist in turning the attacker's hand. Continue twisting his hand to force him to the ground (see Fig. 44-46).

Fig. 44 Pull hand free & turn

Fig. 45 Use 2nd hand to help

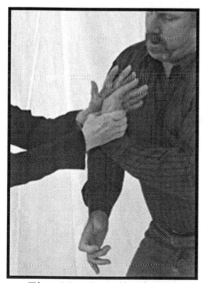

Fig. 45A Detail of turn

Fig. 46 Force to ground

This is a more difficult technique because it starts behind the back. It helps to start the countermove before the attacker has time to settle in and get a really good grip. Practice is necessary to become proficient and be able to execute these moves when necessary. So remember – practice, practice.

Let's look at another example of how a wrist lock turn might be used, in this case a front two hand throat choke. While I feel any throat choke is a serious threat justifying a strong response up to and including Level III, we are going to use the wrist lock turn to deal with the attacker in this example. I want to emphasize that while this is a Level I technique, it is very powerful and can be used to defeat a variety of attacks.

If he grabs your throat, REACT INSTANTLY since you only have a few seconds before your air and blood supply are cut off. Choose one of his hands and apply the wrist lock turn technique to it. Reach up placing all four fingers on the fleshy part of his thumb, with your thumb towards the knuckle of his little finger. Pull his thumb free from your throat (see Fig. 47-48).

 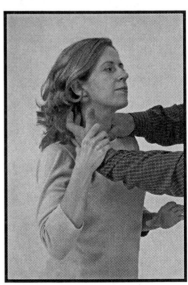

Fig. 47 Thumb on back   Fig. 48 Pry off & turn

Immediately place your other hand on your thumb and keep twisting the wrist, taking your attacker to the ground (see Fig. 49-50).

If he is holding your throat firmly, you may need to distract him by stomping his toes, kneeing him in the groin, or jabbing the fingers of your free hand into his throat or eyes before you can fully pry his hand loose.

Continue this turn strongly to make him go to the ground and escape as soon as possible to safety. If the wrist lock turn is done quickly, and violently, it becomes a Level II technique potentially breaking the attacker's wrist.

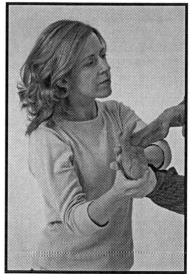 

Fig. 49 Use 2nd hand   Fig. 50 Continue turning

I strongly recommend you add both the wrist release and wrist lock turn techniques to your arsenal. Practice both techniques until you are very familiar with them.

Level II

A Level II response will likely cause pain and possibly injury. The more serious the perceived threat, the higher level of response you want to use to ensure your safety. We're going to learn now how to apply kicks and strikes to neutralize threats to your well being.

Side Kick

While skilled martial artists have many different types of kicks, we are going to concentrate on only one; the side kick (see Fig. 51-54). This kick is executed by first lifting the knee of your front leg, while at the same time turning sideways to your attacker and then forcefully driving your foot into his knee, with the impact point being the bottom of your foot. A strong kick will take his balance and put him on the ground. If

63

you are being seriously threatened, your intention should be to drive your foot ***completely through his knee*** so that he is unable to continue to attack you. The knee is vulnerable to a strong blow, resulting in ligament damage, making it difficult for your attacker to stand or walk. The back leg can be used in the same manner, but because the back leg takes longer to get to the target, this kick is easier to block.

Fig. 51 Ready

Fig. 52 Raise knee

Fig. 53 Pivot

Fig. 54 Kick strongly

In Level I, we learned to use the wrist roll escape. Now someone might say, "Alright, but what happens if he uses two hands to grab my wrist?" No problem. In fact it's better because now both of his hands are occupied holding your wrist, and he isn't going to hit you. Execute a strong side kick into his knee, taking his balance (see Fig. 55-57). He will let go on his way to the ground, and you can go to safety.

Fig. 55 Two hand grab

Fig. 56 Draw leg back

Each strike or kick should be delivered with the loudest yell you can accomplish. Yelling does two things; first it helps focus your energy so that you deliver stronger blows and secondly it helps distract the assailant. The brain likes to deal with one thing at a time and when it is sorting out the yell, it is not responding as quickly to block the incoming kick or strike.

Fig. 57 Kick strongly

65

Note: when you practice with a friend do not actually kick your friend's knee, only make the motion towards the knee or perhaps lightly place the foot on the knee at the extension of the side kick.

Knee Strike

The legs are very powerful and can deliver strong blows using the knee or feet. The knee is going to be our next selected weapon. The knee can be used effectively against the groin, thigh, or other targets. Although everyone knows about using a knee to the groin, that target is not always available or a good choice. If you have a clear shot at the groin, take it because it can be a debilitating blow. However, you should know several things:

- Because little boys from the time they were on the playground learned about getting hit in the groin, it is second nature for a man to quickly protect this part of his anatomy.
- Men value this part of their anatomy highly. Any attempt to hurt it will likely result in the man getting extremely angry. The result may be a robbery turned into a severe beating or worse.
- Recognize when you attempt to harm the groin the stakes go up. However, if you have a clear shot or the situation is desperate, do not hesitate - go for the groin with all the force you can muster. The groin kick can be very effective after performing another technique. The defenses against an attack that we will discuss will use the groin strike in combination with other techniques.

There are other targets for a knee strike. It can be very effective if struck forcefully against the side of the thigh. If the assailant is leaning over, target the stomach or face.

Fig. 58 To the groin

Fig. 59 To the stomach

After you read the description of each strike or kick, stop reading and practice the technique for a few minutes. It is important to learn these self-defense techniques we discuss since they will be used repeatedly to deal with attackers in various situations. Practice, practice, practice to get familiar with all the techniques so they become automatic and you can execute them without thinking.

Palm Strike

The palm strike can be devastating and is an especially good strike for women to use because it has a lot of force. You hit with the heel of the hand, targeting the chin of your assailant (see Fig. 60-63).

Start with your hand low next to your body and slightly above your waist. Drive your palm towards your assailant's chin. The path should be towards his stomach and then curving up to the chin so he doesn't see it coming. You can add more power to the strike by turning your hips towards him at the same time as you deliver the strike. This adds the extra power of your turning body. Drive the heel of your hand strongly into his chin using all of the force and power you can muster.

To even make the strike more powerful, sink slightly at the knees and rise up as you deliver the strike. This makes use of the bounce

67

energy developed as you sink down and then rise up. Properly delivered, this technique will literally lift him off his feet. Yell as you deliver this strike.

Fig. 60 Grabbed

Fig. 61 Hand towards chin

Fig. 62 Palm to chin

Fig. 63 Drive through

Front Throat Choke

This example of using a palm strike is to stop an attacker trying to choke you. As the attacker reaches forward to attempt the choke, execute a powerful palm strike to the chin. As he gets close, keep your hand near his stomach and arch it upwards so he doesn't see it coming (see Fig. 64-66). Drive the palm of your hand through his chin in a powerful blow.

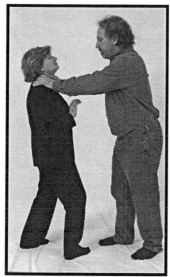
Fig. 64 Grabbed

Fig. 65 Palm to chin

Fig. 66 Knee to groin

If necessary, finish with a knee to the groin or a side kick to his knee. Remember to utilize more than one technique to defeat an attacker.

Elbow Strike

The elbow is a short range weapon, but it can deliver an extremely powerful blow (see Fig. 67-70). Deliver this strike by driving the point of the elbow like a battering ram into your opponent or swing it sideways so the side of the elbow impacts your target. The elbow can also be swung upwards to contact the chin. To add more force to the blow, cover the hand on the arm of the striking elbow with your other hand, using the second hand to add force to drive the elbow deeper into your target.

Primary points of interest on your assailant are the solar plexus, chin, face, side of head, but any other part of his body you can reach with your elbow is appropriate. Obviously if he is really tall you might not be able to reach his head with your elbow. In that case, target the solar plexus or go with a side kick or a palm strike.

Fig. 67 To solar plexus

Fig. 68 To face

Fig. 69 To chin   Fig. 70 To side of face

Back Bear Hug – Arms Free

If someone bear hugs you from the back (arms are free), immediately stomp his foot, turn slightly sideways and drive your elbow into his face. Immediately turn the other way and drive the other elbow into his head. Keep alternating elbow strikes until he releases you (see Fig. 71-77).

Fig. 71 Grabbed   Fig. 72 Raise foot   Fig. 73 Heel into foot

Fig. 74 Elbow to face

Fig. 75 Turn & elbow again

Fig. 76 Elbow again

Fig. 77 Kick knee

If he buries his head tightly into your back you may not be effective with the elbow strikes. It that case pry one of his fingers loose and bend it backwards to break it (see next technique). This will normally get him to release you. If he then continues to come towards you, execute a side kick to the knee and/or a palm strike to the chin.

Back Bear Hug – Arms Pinned

This defensive tactic uses prying back one of the attacker's fingers (see Fig. 78-81) to achieve the release. First stomp his foot or use the back of your head to his face to distract him. At the same, time pry loose one of his fingers and bend it back strongly. Continue to bend his finger, forcing him to release you. Turn and kick strongly to his knee.

Fig. 78 Stomp foot

Fig. 79 Pry finger loose

Fig. 80 Pull finger away

Fig. 81 Kick to knee

Back Bear Hug – Arms Pinned 2

A second method of dealing with an attack from the back is to drive the back of your head sharply into his nose. Immediately totally relax, sinking down quickly at the knees while at the same time flaring your elbows out and up like you are going to fly. This should cause his arms to go up over your shoulders freeing you (see Fig. 82-86).

Fig. 82 Grabbed

Fig. 83 Back of head to nose

Fig. 84 Flare arms & sink

Fig. 85 Strike to the groin

Immediately execute a knife hand strike to the groin by powerfully swinging your arm past your knee and let the arc continue with the knife hand impacting the groin. You may choose to turn slightly and execute a side kick to the knee.

Fig. 86 Side kick to knee

Front Throat Choke

This defense against a throat choke uses an arm sweep and an elbow strike to break the choke hold. When your throat is grabbed, *immediately* sweep one arm over both his arms and turn with your sweeping arm so your back is now to him (see Fig. 87-90). It doesn't make any difference which arm you choose to sweep over both of his, just quickly sweep one arm over. It is the turning of the body that adds power allowing you to break his hold.

Fig. 87 Grabbed

Fig. 88 Arm over

Fig. 89 Continue over

Fig. 90 Trap his arms

Clamp your sweeping arm close to your side, trapping his arms and continue by leaning slightly forward while sinking down at the knees. This will cause a tall assailant to bend over, putting his head in range of your elbow when swung in a backward arc. Drive your sweeping arm elbow forcefully into his face. Finish with a side kick to the knee or palm strike to the chin (see Fig. 91-92).

Fig. 91 Elbow   Fig. 92 Side kick to knee

Front Bear Hug – Arms Pinned

If someone bear hugs you from the front, pinning your arms, strike his nose with the top of your forehead. Bring your forehead sharply into his nose and keep striking it like a hammer driving a nail into wood. Use your fingers to grab a fold of skin and then twist it hard, like turning a key, which will cause a very painful pinch. Target the rib area or the underside of the upper arm, the triceps. Use the knees to strike the groin area. Stomp his toes. Use your teeth on anything you can bite, especially the throat. Your life is at stake so don't be squeamish. Keep doing everything until he releases you and you can escape. If he starts to come towards again, you can execute a palm strike to the chin or side kick to the knee.

Fig. 93 Grabbed

Fig. 94 Head into nose

Fig. 95 Note the pinch.

Fig. 96 Knee to the groin

Wrists grabbed from behind

A method of dealing with an attacker that grabs both your wrists from behind is to totally relax your arms. The key to this technique is to *totally* relax your arms and let them go limp. Your normal reaction will be to try to pull away and fight the grab. Remember, never fight force with force because your attacker will most likely be bigger and stronger - you will not win that contest. Instead, completely relax your arms, and slide back towards your attacker while at the same time turning sideways and bringing your hand towards your navel. Then immediately execute a knife hand strike to the groin followed by an elbow strike to the solar plexus or face. Finish by kicking his knee (see Fig. 97-102).

Fig. 97 Grabbed

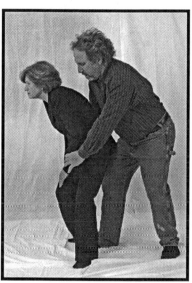

Fig. 98 Relax & begin turn

Fig. 99 Groin strike

Fig. 100 Elbow strike

Fig. 101 Raise knee   Fig. 102 Kick knee

This technique must be tried with a partner to fully appreciate how initially relaxing and not fighting the grab makes it effective

Grab From Behind – One Arm Throat Choke

If someone grabs you from behind with one arm around your throat and the other arm holding one of your arms, *immediately* turn your chin, tucking your chin bone into the crook of his elbow, to allowing you space to breathe. This is important because you have only seconds to react to keep your carotid arteries and windpipe from being squeezed shut. Use your free hand to grab the choking arm to pry it away. Stomp his toes to distract him, and at the same time bring the hand that he is holding, up as if you are executing a palm strike to someone in front of you or visualize lifting a can of soda up in front of you. Immediately back out under your upraised arm. You should be able to back out under your arm, pulling your head free. Quickly execute a side kick forcefully to the side or back of his knee to put him on the ground (see Fig. 103-107). Be prepared for him to get up, so run like crazy. If there is no time, deliver another kick or palm strike. Like all of the techniques, this escape has to be done quickly and without hesitation.

Fig. 103 Grabbed

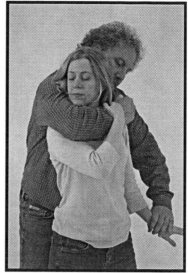

Fig. 104 Chin to elbow

Fig. 105 Raise arm

Fig. 106 Back under arm

Fig. 107 Kick to the knee

Punch or Grab Deflections

We discussed earlier never to meet force with force, rather get out of the way if at all possible, and take the necessary defensive action. If an attacker throws a punch or attempts to grab you, you can use a deflection rather than trying to block the punch or grab. The deflection works by bringing your hand up in a circular motion as if you are smoothing the hair on the side of your head. It is not necessary to knock the attacker's hand away. Just bring your hand up, contacting his wrist or forearm and then brush your hair by your ear while keeping his hand on the outside of your hand. Another way to describe this motion is like bringing your hand up to salute and then continuing the circular motion past your ear. He will miss you. Note that you are not trying to knock his hand away; you are merely guiding it safely past you.

The first deflection is an inside deflection, which occurs when you deflect the attack, but are still in front of the attacker (see Fig. 108-111). The woman in this case deflects the attack and then can respond with a palm strike, a throat strike or a knee to the groin. Especially note in Fig. 109-110 how the woman's hand guides the attacker's grabbing hand safely past her head allowing her to deliver the counterstrike.

Fig. 108 Grab attempt

Fig. 109 Raise hand up

Fig. 110 Palm strike

Fig. 111 Throat strike

An outside deflection occurs when you move outside his attack and are no longer directly in front of him, but rather to the side. This is the preferred position. As you see the punch or grab coming, slide out of the way by going to the outside or offline. Intercept his arm at the wrist with your hand by bringing it up in the circular motion. Keep your hand in contact with the attacker's wrist and guide it past your head. Respond with a kick to the knee (see Fig. 112-115).

Fig. 112 Punch coming   Fig. 113 Intercept punch

Note again how the woman's hand guides the punch safely past her head in Fig. 113-114 before responding with a kick to put the attacker on the ground.

Fig. 114 Guide to outside   Fig. 115 Counter with kick to knee

Level III

Level III responses are designed to respond to the most serious threats where you believe your life or physical safety or someone else's are in jeopardy. These responses can cause serious injury and *may be lethal* if applied with enough force. Any strike to the throat has the potential to result in serious injury or death and should be reserved for the most threatening situations. Let's look at Level III responses and how to apply them.

Circle Hand Strike

The Circle Hand Strike is sometimes referred to as the tiger mouth strike. The fingers are extended tightly together and the thumb extended at roughly a 90 degree angle forming a "rounded L" as you look at the thumb and index finger. The fingers will be slightly curved as if you are trying to grip a large tree trunk. This strike is delivered in a similar manner to the palm strike, only the target is the throat (see Fig. 116-119).

The impact point on the hand should be the web of the hand or halfway between the tip of the thumb and tip of the index finger. A strong strike to the throat will cause immediate pain and possible breathing problems for your assailant. Delivered with enough force it can crush the windpipe and *may be lethal.* This technique should only be used when your physical well being is being severely threatened.

Fig. 116 Grabbed

Fig. 117 Target throat

Fig. 118 Impact throat

Fig. 119 Drive through

Knife Hand Strike

The knife hand is formed by bringing the fingers tightly together and the thumb is held close to the first knuckle. The target of this strike is the front or side of the throat (see Fig. 120-121). It can be delivered in two different manners. The backhand starts with the thumb close to your chest, the palm facing down, and makes a horizontal cutting motion to your attacker's throat.

Fig. 120 Ready your hand

Fig. 121 Strike throat

The second method starts with the hand by your ear and makes a chopping motion to the side of the neck (see Fig. 122-124). Strike the side of the neck as though you intend for your hand to go entirely through the neck, like an axe chopping through a log.

Fig. 122 Hand ready

Fig. 123 To side of neck

Fig. 124 Strike forcefully

Tap your own throat lightly to check the effectiveness of these strikes. Now think of what it might feel like it you hit this area with force.

The effects to the front of the throat were already discussed in the circle hand strike. When the side of the throat is struck, the carotid arteries are affected. They can spasm, constrict and cause unconsciousness, or in some cases *cause death.* Any strike to the throat must be done with the knowledge that serious damage can be done *including death,* so these strikes should be reserved for the most serious situations. If you miss the carotids, it will still likely have a stunning effect. Another target for the knife hand strike is the temple of the assailant. A strong blow here will stun the individual and a very forceful blow *can be lethal.*

Eagle Claw Strike

This hand strike starts by spreading your curved fingers apart as if you are holding a softball. Imagine the talons of an eagle getting ready to strike. The target is the eyes. You deliver this strike as if you are pushing the softball into your assailant's face, with the fingers targeting the eyes (Fig. 125-126). One of your fingers will get there. A finger jabbed into the eye will cause extreme pain and normally make an attacker think twice about continuing with whatever plans he had. Yell as you deliver the strike.

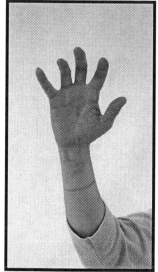

Fig. 125 Fingers ready

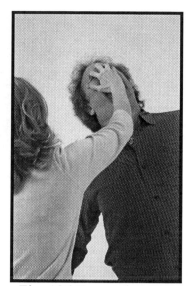

Fig. 126 Target the eyes

Eye Gouge

The eyes are very vulnerable targets. The eye gouge can be extremely effective because it causes severe pain and the assailant is generally not expecting it. You need to immediately get past the reluctance to put your thumb into their eye. When your life is being threatened, you need to respond with whatever it takes to defend yourself. Grab his head to control it so he can't jerk it away. Wrap one arm around his head and hug it to your shoulder to immobilize it. Then take your free hand thumb and shove it into his eye as deeply as you can (see Fig. 127-128).

Fig. 127 Grabbed   Fig. 128 Thumb into eye

The eye gouge causes excruciating pain and he will try to jerk his head away. Hold on tight and continue gouging until he releases you. The intense pain will normally induce him to release you immediately and he will back away holding his eye. You can follow up with a kick to the knee or groin if necessary and make your escape.

It should be noted that thrusting your thumb deeply into the eye can cause *severe damage and potentially blindness*, but if your life is being threatened you may have to take this serious action.

Some example situations of when you might utilize this technique would be if someone bear hugs you from the front leaving your arms free, if someone is trying to sexually assault you, or any other serious situation where your arms are free and you can reach the attackers head.

Handling Other Situations

If you are knocked to the ground, immediately try to get back on your feet. If this isn't feasible, turn over on your back like an upside down turtle so that you can defend yourself (see Fig. 129). *This is important*. If you remain on your stomach you are very vulnerable to the attacker getting on your back and choking you. When you are on your back you are protecting your spine. Tuck your chin down to protect your throat, bring your arms up over your chest, hands by your head and use your legs to kick the attacker's knee. Pivot on your back so that your legs are always facing him. Every time he moves to the side, pivot your body to keep your legs always towards him. Wait till he is close and kick powerfully to his knee (see Fig.130). Do not stick your leg out in an attempt to keep him back. He will grab it and a weak kick will just alert him to your intentions. Be patient, wait until he is close and then kick like releasing a powerful piston driving your foot through his knee.

Fig. 129 Defensive position

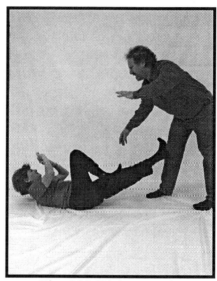

Fig. 130 Kick strongly

Get back up on your feet as soon as you can since you will be able to defend yourself better standing up and then escape at the first chance.

If you are by a car or other large object, you can keep the object between you and the attacker. You can run around a car, keeping your attacker on the other side. As he comes to one side, you scoot to the other. You should be screaming and attracting as much attention as possible while doing this.

Most of the time I advise you to make a decision on what to do based on the specific circumstances. However, if someone attempts to force you into a car, **DO NOT** get in the car voluntarily. He may display a weapon and threaten to shoot you or cut you with a knife. He may say he won't hurt you if you get in the car and just do what he wants. If he is prepared to shoot or hurt you in the middle of a mall parking lot, think of what he is ready to do to you on a lonely road. He wants to get you in the car to isolate you away from any witnesses and take you where someone can't hear you. You do not want to go from crime scene #1 to crime scene #2. The statistics of survival are simply not good if you get in a car. Better to be shot or cut in the parking lot where you might get help. Run in a zigzag pattern if he has a gun. The odds of someone being able to hit a running target are 4 out of 100 and even then it likely will not be a vital hit. If you stand still the odds of being hit are very high.

If you can't run or fight because you are being held and are being dragged to a car, let your legs go slack, become dead weight and drop to the pavement. I normally advocate staying on your feet since this gives you the best opportunity to defend yourself, however I am going to discuss this exception. In a situation where someone is trying to force you into a car and nothing is working, sink to the ground. When you are standing on your feet it doesn't take much force to drag you along since you are supporting most of your weight. However, if you just relax and sink down to the ground, he now has to pull all of your weight (see Fig. 131-132).

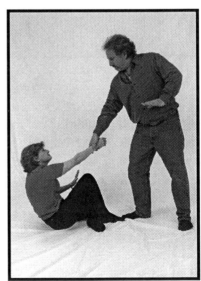

Fig. 131 Grabbed   Fig. 132 Go limp & sit

It suddenly becomes a hard task and you are not going anywhere unless he physically tries to pick you up. You should use ground defense tactics kicking his knees and clawing his eyes to make this task very difficult.

Please note: this tactic is good in a crowded parking lot of a shopping mall, but is not good on a lonely road. It is a very good *delaying tactic* if help is nearby. Again, you will **normally always want to stay on your feet to better defend yourself.** However, this can be used if help is nearby and as a last ditch defense against being shoved into a car.

Do not voluntarily allow yourself to be restrained with handcuffs, tape, rope or any other means. If you are restrained, your options go down and your chance of physical harm increases dramatically.

If you do find yourself in the car, you *must escape.* Try to do this before the car gains much speed. Claw his eyes, jerk the wheel, jump out, do whatever is necessary to escape. If you are placed in the trunk of the car, feel around the inside of the trunk toward the latch since cars now (since 2002) have a trunk release inside the trunk specifically for someone who is trapped in the trunk. The thought was primarily for children, who inadvertently lock themselves in while playing, but it will work just as well for you. You can use your cell phone. You can kick out the taillights and try to stick something out like a hand or piece of clothing to attract attention. Failing that, at least rip the wires off, rendering the taillights inoperable and hopefully attracting the attention of law enforcement.

Multiple Attackers

When you are faced with multiple attackers do not let them surround you. You must move immediately to the outside of them. In this case you (Y) are surrounded by attacker 1 (A_1) and attacker 2 (A_2). Move quickly to get around attacker 2 so that A_1 is now behind A_2. Use a palm strike or knee kick to put A_2 on the ground and then deal with A_1. Moving to the outside of the group allows you to deal with one attacker at a time.

$$\overset{\rightarrow \quad \rightarrow \quad \rightarrow \quad \rightarrow}{A_1 \quad Y \quad A_2 \quad \downarrow} \qquad\qquad A_1 \quad A_2 \leftarrow Y$$

93

Use the same tactics for more than two. Get to the outside, deal with the closest one, keep moving, and deal with the next one. Don't just push them away; when they get close, really nail them to put them on the ground. You want them out of the fight. Do not become a stationary target; you must keep moving, circling to the outside. Their interest in you will likely go down once one or two of them can't get up off the ground. Escape to safety at the first opportunity.

Practice

You will want to reread this chapter several times to become familiar with the techniques. Do not be discouraged if you are not able to do all of the techniques immediately. Each time you review them they will become more familiar and easier to execute. I strongly encourage you to get with a partner and practice these basic self-defense moves so that you become proficient. You will note that we used the same strikes, kick and turns to deal with various attacks. It is important to become proficient in these basic moves, which have been specifically selected for their effectiveness. Practice applying these techniques against the various attacks. Start slowly and as you gain expertise you can begin to go faster with your partner. Exercise restraint because these techniques will hurt if you apply them too strongly to your partner. They do need to be put on with enough force so that there is some pain to demonstrate their effectiveness and verify your understanding. Agree with your partner that if the technique gets too painful, they will slap their thigh or chest and you should *immediately release them*. They should practice the techniques on you so you feel the force and understand how the techniques work. Practice routinely so you can use the techniques without hesitation. If you have any health issues, you may wish to consult your physician before beginning practice.

This book does not attempt to discuss how to disarm attackers with weapons. Defense against weapons is in the category of advanced techniques. You must become proficient in dealing with unarmed assailants before training to deal with weapons. The consequences of a poorly applied technique against someone with a weapon can be extremely serious. Dealing with weapons will be discussed in a future women's advanced self-defense book.

Let's review **Action**:

✓ Use Verbal Self-Defense.
✓ Decide if it is to be Fight or Flight.
✓ Your body is a virtual arsenal of weapons.
✓ Decide what level of response is appropriate to the threat.
✓ Never meet force with force. Slide off from the direct line of contact.
✓ Work against the assailant's thumb to escape grasps.
✓ Use multiple kicks and strikes to persuade attacker to cease.
✓ Yell while doing all the techniques – first to focus your power and secondly to distract him.
✓ React instantly to any attempt to choke you.
✓ First become proficient in these techniques then add the rest:

o Wrist release	o Side kick
o Wrist lock turn	o Palm strike

✓ Practice the techniques with a partner.
✓ DO NOT GET in a car.
✓ Stay on your feet and only use ground defense when absolutely necessary.
✓ Get to the outside of multiple attackers and deal with each, one at a time.
✓ Practice, practice, practice until the techniques become very familiar.

The physical self-defense techniques that were covered above are further illustrated in a DVD. The information regarding this DVD may be obtained at www.livingsafelytoday.com or www.seesallykickass.com.

Chapter 5

Preventing Sexual Assault

A woman's deepest fear may be that of being sexually violated by a stranger. When I talk with women about what scares them, this is the answer I get most often. We're going to discuss ways to reduce the probability of that happening.

The very simplified definition of rape is forced sexual intercourse with penetration using physical or psychological intimidation. Sexual Assault is any unwanted sexual contact. Each state has its own specific legal definition.

A woman has a 1 in 6 probability of being a victim of a rape or attempted rape in her lifetime. 83% of rapes are to women less than 25 years old. (Source: *Prevalence, Incidence and Consequences of Violence Against Women Survey* – National Institute of Justice and Center for Disease Control and Prevention 1998)

Rape is one of the most under reported crimes because of the victim feeling shame, being in denial, not wanting it to be public, feeling intimidated, believing it was her fault, or being drugged. Asa Hutchinson, Administrator of the Drug Enforcement Administration, testified on October 10, 2002, before the House Judiciary Subcommittee on Crime, Terrorism and Homeland Security, stating that only 32 of 100 rapes are actually reported to the police and that 15 to 20% of all rapes were facilitated by drugs.

While rapists can be subdivided into a number of categories, I have elected to describe them as two broad general categories of rapists:

- Acquaintance – 70%
  - o He wants power and reassurance.
  - o He uses coercion and threat of violence.
  - o He doesn't believe his behavior is rape.
  - o He thinks the victim had a good time. This person will force himself on you then afterward say, "I had a really good time. Let's do this again next Saturday night."

- Stranger – 30%
  - o He wants to assert power and is domineering.
  - o He may be retaliating against women.
  - o He may have anger and is excited by violence.
  - o A small segment of stranger rapists kill their victims and are therefore very, very dangerous.

The majority of the time you are likely to encounter the *acquaintance rapist*. The Department of Justice's Bureau of Justice Statistics for 2003 estimates that 70% of rapes are committed by males that the woman knew or was acquainted with such as friends, neighbors, relatives, and co-workers.

While there is more publicity about stranger rape, you are in fact three to four times more likely to be faced with acquaintance or date rape. This is an issue since most women are concerned about stranger rape, but dismiss or deny the risk of date or acquaintance rape, when that is the bigger threat. The motives that you are most likely to deal with are the man's desire for power and control, and the desire for sex when the consent is not given.

First, it is appropriate to reiterate that you alone determine when and with whom you want to have sexual relations. Second, you can say "NO" at any time, no matter how far things have progressed, and after that it is rape. Third, state laws require that explicit consent must be freely given, and in most states that consent cannot be obtained if the woman is drunk or otherwise incapacitated. Men cannot legally engage in intercourse unless explicit consent has been given.

Who are most at risk and the most likely victims of date rape?

- College freshmen
  - This is usually the first time they are away from their parents on an extended protracted basis.
  - Experiencing "freedom" for the first time may cause them to drink more, making them *substantially* more vulnerable.
  - They want to be accepted by their new friends and may "go along" with the crowd.
  - They have false sense of security because crime on college campuses is typically under reported. In fact, only about 5% of rapes and sexual assaults on college campuses are reported.
  - Typically college freshmen do not know the reputations of fraternities or males she makes acquaintances or parties with.
  - All of these things combined substantially increase the threat level to the college freshmen. As you might suspect, the first few months put her at the highest risk. Early on, she may go places and do things that later on she would not, after gaining more information and experience.

- Older women
  - They can be lonely and are searching for companionship. As a result, they may lower their normal standards or take risks they typically wouldn't.
  - They can be overconfident, believing they have been through the dating game and are experienced. A "been there, done that" sort of attitude, minimizing any potential danger.
  - They search in bars and personal ads looking for "Mr. Right."

College women are identified as especially at risk. A 2004 study conducted at 119 schools by the Harvard School of Public Health Alcohol Study, St. Joseph's University and the University of Arizona reported 1 in 20 (5%) being raped. Seventy five percent of those said they were intoxicated at the time. The problem with getting accurate numbers is admitting (understanding) a crime was committed and the failure to report it. Ninety five percent of rapes on campuses go unreported. You can check any major university's website for safety statistics and find that very few rapes, usually less that ten, are reported.

A university that has 20,000 students, with 50% female, statistically (using 5% and four years) should have about 125 cases of rape per year.

Date rape proceeds in a series of small steps. Each time the man doesn't get rejection or told "No," he assumes that means approval and he proceeds further. It may start with hand holding, then a kiss, then deeper kissing, then caressing and attempts to go further.

There is the old saying, "Men will give love for sex, and women give sex for love." This highlights the way some men and women see sex differently. Some men see sex as sport. A typical comment that a college man might make to his fraternity buddies after returning from a date is, "I scored!" Note that he did not say, "I had a loving, intimate moment with someone I really care about," or another similar sentiment. An analogy to how the man thinks would be a football game. There is the kickoff when he picks up his date. During the progress of the date, he holds her hand and is on the 20 yard line. He puts his hand on her shoulder and then is on the 30 yard line; he kisses her lightly and now is on the 40 yard line. He kisses her more passionately and is over the midfield line. He puts his hand under her blouse to caress her, and now he only has 30 yards to go to "score." If his date stops him, then he is put back on his own 20 yard line and has to start over again on his campaign to "score."

It is important for you to understand how date rape progresses in order to stop it early and prevent something more serious from happening. You should set the expectations early, as clearly as possible to minimize any misunderstandings. Better to overstate your thoughts than to risk having any ambiguity.

How To Protect Yourself

- Have a roommate. Single women who live alone are at a significantly higher risk.
- Get some information on anyone who is interested in dating you. Ask around about his reputation. What type of guy is he really? Does he drink too much, talk negatively about women, show bully or domineering tendencies? Have other girls had problems with him? The same goes for any fraternity parties you are

invited to. Check before you go. What is the reputation of the fraternity? If it is lots of alcohol and aggressive men, take a pass and go to safer environments to have fun.

- If he has a much more liberal attitude towards sex than you do, he will assume you think the way he does since you are going out with him. Associate with people that have the same values as you.

- Be especially wary of athletes, particularly stars, who may feel a sense of entitlement and the idea that the rules don't apply to them. In the same manner, be very careful about certain college sports parties where there is a lot of drinking. By definition, these activities will have a high population of potentially problem individuals. Many collegiate groups of athletes have an "Animal House" kind of attitude. Consider very carefully before attending any of these parties and recognize these are risky places to have fun. Another category of potential problems is men in powerful positions used to getting their way, such as executives, business owners or other men in power positions. In the old days of Hollywood it was called the "casting couch." Sometimes sons assume they deserve some sort of entitlement just because their dad has influence. Sexual harassment lawsuits have gone a long way to reducing this problem, but it still exists.

- Have the first date in a public place in the daytime. Drive your own car or meet him there. Consider taking along a friend or double dating. Lots of people = safety.

- Introduce your date to your roommate, parents or friends, and explain where you are going and when you expect to return.

- Wear appropriate clothes for how you want the situation or date to go. The lower the cut of the blouse, the more sheer the material, or the higher the skirt, the more attention you'll get from your date. That level of notice may or may not be what you want. You may want to be careful about unknowingly reinforcing any ideas that he might have. Now I acknowledge you should be able to wear whatever you want and not be subject to aggression. You are absolutely correct on that point, but at the same time you wouldn't think of going down the street waving a handful of cash. Use discretion.

- Communicate early and often about your expectations. Examples would be, "I'm not interested in a physical relationship," "I don't drink or do drugs," "I just want to be friends," "I expect you to respect my wishes." You get the idea.

- Paying your own way prevents him from spending a lot of money and expecting something in return.

- Listen carefully to him. What is his attitude toward women? If he speaks negatively about them, believes they are a tease or believes they are really responsible for a man's behavior, it is time to head for the exit.

- If you are uncomfortable, ask to be taken home, or go home separately by calling a friend or taxi. Trust your instincts and sixth sense. If it doesn't feel right, it is time to leave.

- *Always take your cell phone with you.* Go to the ladies' room to make your call if there is a problem. Have a backup plan if the date is a problem. You can arrange for a friend to call you midway through the date and use the phone call as reason to terminate the date if you are uncomfortable.

- Don't let yourself be isolated. Don't go with him to his place or other isolated spots, and don't let yourself be isolated with a group of men at a party. Stay in public places and with friends, or at least in mixed groups. The more isolated, the more dangerous, and the more likely your date might become more aggressive. "Isolated" can be a private room at a fraternity, alone on the beach, in his parked car or by the way, your apartment.

- If he drinks too much or does drugs, it is time for you to leave. Refuse to get drunk or take drugs. Go home a separate way since you do not need to be driven home by a drunk driver.

- Alcohol is one of the tools of rapists. They use alcohol to lower inhibitions and reduce the victim's ability to resist their advances. Beware of anyone that is trying to get you to drink more than you want to or should.

- If you are going to drink, drink in moderation. Make a drink last a long time. Eating food and drinking other liquids will help lessen the impact of an alcoholic drink. If you are drunk, you are at *significantly* higher risk of having a very serious problem with your date or other men.

- If you are at a party where too much alcohol is flowing and lots of people are becoming drunk, it is time to leave. Sticking around means you just get to spend more quality time with progressively drunker people who may become alcohol aggressive.

- Whatever you say must be consistent with your body language or he will get a mixed message and assume the more liberal interpretation.

- Do not let him come in when he says, "I promise I'll only have one drink and go," or a similar gambit. Don't accept any excuse to stay such as, "I've had too much to drink, can I just sleep on your couch?" The answer is, "NO! I will call you a cab." Agreeing to any such requests will isolate you with him and the risks go up.

Alcohol is the first set of tools that rapists use and the second set is date rape drugs. Date rape drugs, which cause loss of inhibition and memory, are more prevalent than most people realize. The victim may not be aware she ingested the drug since there is no smell and, while slightly salty tasting, it can be difficult to detect when mixed with other liquids such as soda, juices or beer. Every year there are a number of deaths, associated with date rape drugs. They are a serious problem. The three most common are the following:

- **Rohypnol** – referred to as Mexican valium, roofies, rope, R-2, and RZ. Normally an oblong green tablet, this can be crushed and put in a drink, causing drowsiness, dizziness, confusion, loss of inhibition, and amnesia. The manufacturer now puts a dye in the drug which will show up if mixed in a drink, but generic versions may not have the dye.

- **GHB** or gamma hydroxyl butyrate – referred to as Liquid Ecstasy, Liquid X, Easy Lay, Scoop, Goop and Georgia Home Boy. GHB can either be a liquid or white powder that mixes easily with a drink quickly causing dizziness, drowsiness, nausea, unconsciousness, amnesia, seizures, lowered heart rate, and respiratory failure. It renders the person incapable of resisting, and causes memory problems. Overdoses require immediate medical intervention. The DEA estimates there were 71 deaths due to GHB by November 2000.

- **Ketamine** – referred to as Special K, Super K, green, cat Valium, jet and super acid. It can be a clear liquid or white to off white powder causing mental confusion and loss of coordination. There can be other serious reactions since it is related to PCP.

In 1996 Congress passed The Drug-Induced Rape Prevention & Punishment Act. It is a federal offense to commit a crime of violence including rape by administering controlled substances without the victim's consent or knowledge. The date rape drugs mentioned above are covered by this law. Federal penalties include up to 20 years of imprisonment.

Date Rape Drug Prevention

- Volunteer to make your own drinks. Better yet, open a bottled or canned beverage. Watch carefully, if a bottled or canned product is opened for you, to insure it doesn't get adulterated. If someone else makes your drink, carefully watch it being made. If your drink tastes funny, spill it. Never drink out of a common punch bowl mix or drink something someone has passed to you. While you normally think that only alcoholic drinks might contain date rape drugs, it can be any drinks, including soda or fruit juice.

- Don't ever leave your drink unattended. Have a very trustworthy friend watch it or take it with you, even if it is to the ladies' room. You can always wash off the bottom of the glass if you have to put the glass on the floor of the bathroom stall, but the hazards of date rape drugs are permanent.

- If you think your drink has been spiked, get out and seek help immediately. Tell medical personnel you think you may have been drugged. There are tests for the presence of these drugs.

- Make a pact and agree with trusted friends that if any of you ever appear drunk or otherwise impaired, that you will stay with each other, get help and insure that person gets safely home.

- If you become aware of anyone using date rape drugs, you should take action by spilling the contaminated drinks, helping anyone under the influence of the drug, and reporting the crime to the police. You may save the life of the intended target, and at the very least, you have likely prevented them from being sexually assaulted.

To summarize two key points: *don't drink and don't become isolated.* These two precautions alone will significantly reduce your risk of being a victim of sexual assault.

So now, you have taken all of the precautions outlined above, but your date has been lots of fun and you really like the guy. You start kissing and suddenly you find he is getting very aggressive. He clearly wants sex and you don't. What do you do?

- You need to get things slowed down quickly. Call a halt to any further progress and stop giving any affection to ensure there is no misunderstanding your message. Your body language must match your words.

- Tell him to stop immediately! Take his hands away and button back up. The sooner you do this the better. The longer it goes on, the less serious he believes you are in really wanting him to stop. Some men believe that the woman really wants to have sex, but think she is just saying "no" because that is what is expected of her. He needs to understand "no" means "NO!"

- Sometimes a man thinks "no" means try harder. He remembers as a little boy when he wanted a cookie and was told "no," if he persisted, he was finally given the cookie. Do not allow him to continue pressuring you. "No" means "No" and "Stop!"

- Do not let your date coerce you into having sex by saying things like, "If you really loved me, you would....," "You've got me all excited, you can't stop now," "I'll only go a little way," "I really love you," and well you get the idea. Do not let anyone coerce you into doing something you don't want to do. If he really loves and respects you, he will honor your wishes and not press you.

- Tell him you do not want to have sex, nor do you want to be touched. Be forceful and clear to prevent sending any mixed messages. Make sure that he understands he is responsible for his own behavior.

- Make sure that he understands that you have said "NO" and if he proceeds further, it is rape. Tell him he does not have your consent. You have the right to say "no" at any time no matter how far things have progressed or what you might have said earlier. You have the right to change your mind. Once you say, "no" it's "NO!" Clearly, the sooner a stop is called, the easier it will be to get things calmed down.

- Make sure he understands that if he continues, there will be serious consequences. Don't get into a debate of what those consequences might be. Just say, "I've asked you to stop and you do not have my consent to have sexual relations with me."

- If your date continues to force himself on you, you have to decide to fight or submit. If you decide to resist, you have a good chance of avoiding being sexually assaulted. However, he may be threatening you or there may be other factors that make you decide that resisting is not an appropriate course of action. You have to make that decision at the time.

- If you decide to fight, use the tactics outlined in the chapter on **Action**. Do not hold back. Be his worst nightmare. Get out and away as soon as you can.

Rape is never the victim's fault. The person is not a victim, but a survivor of a violent assault. I urge you to report all rapes and prosecute. It may be embarrassing and possibly humiliating, but your efforts may save someone else. If the individual does *not* suffer consequences, he will continue on to the next victim. Rapists continue to be serial rapists until they are stopped.

Let's take a look at some of the warning signs that a person may be showing too much interest in you.

- He shows too much attention making you feel uncomfortable. If your sixth sense is screaming and the hair is standing up on the back of your neck, pay attention.

- While a little flirting can be fun, be careful when it is someone that you are not interested in, and it continues or intensifies.

- He is constantly hanging around and showing up at odd times without a good reason.

- He makes suggestive comments or otherwise hints he wants to have sex with you.

- He refuses to accept no for an answer or other indications that you are not interested.

- He has hostility and anger to you or women in general.

Other times the warning signs are more difficult and the best defense is to use all of the prevention measures outlined in the **Avoidance** section to avoid being at the wrong place at the wrong time. Trust your sixth sense and instincts.

You have done everything right, but now you find yourself being confronted and threatened with sexual assault. The Bureau of Justice Statistics for 2003 state that 54% of the time when women took self protection measures such as; running, fighting, screaming, resisting, getting help, and persuading, it helped the situation. 32% of the time it neither helped nor hurt and 14% of the time it hurt the situation. This data indicates that taking some action either helped or was neutral 86% of the time. When it helped (54%), 38% of the time injury or greater injury was avoided, 23% of the time it scared the offender away, 23% of the time the intended victim escaped, 10 % of the time other people were protected. *You* have to make the decision on the spot of what to do, but the statistics indicate you should take action.

Action Plan

- Make an instant decision regarding what you need to do. *If you can, immediately bolt and run.* Do not hesitate to flee to safety if there is any opening at all.

- If you can not immediately run, talk with the assailant to try to get him to see you as a person. You might discuss how he would feel if the same thing was happening to his sister or mother. You will have to use your best judgment on the strategy to use. You might throw him off guard by saying, "I have to go to the bathroom first," or some other ploy and then run.

- You can say, "I have AIDS," "I have a raging case of herpes," "I have cancer of the uterus," "I just came back from Africa and I may have the Ebola virus," or anything else that comes to mind. Make up anything you can say that will dissuade a potential assailant. In one case a woman said, "Let's go to my hotel room where we will be more comfortable." When they got to the hotel lobby she screamed and they apprehended the assailant. In another incident the woman said, "I'm busy right now, but let's have a date back here at 7 p.m." The police were waiting for him when he arrived at 7 p.m.

- *Do not say, "I know you," "I'll remember you," or "I'll make sure the police get you."* The assailant may feel threatened so much that he severely hurts or kills you. Don't give the assailant any reason to do further harm to you.

- If you can't run and decide to fight, use the kicks, strikes, and gouges discussed in Chapter 4 - **Action**. Give it 110% and continue until the threat is neutralized or you can escape. Yell loudly as you are doing this. You will probably surprise the assailant, since he will most likely not be expecting a vigorous defense.

- You may pretend to cooperate and then when his defenses are lowered, strike without hesitation.

- Do not allow yourself to be restrained with handcuffs or rope if at all possible. Your options go down dramatically if you are restrained.

- Do remember as much as possible about the assailant, so that you can give the best description possible to the police.

- Make yourself as unattractive as possible. Stick your finger down your throat to induce yourself to vomit. If you do, throw up on yourself and rub it all over you. Urinate and defecate. Again, rub it all over you. This is unappealing, but that is exactly what you want to be to anyone trying to assault you.

- Try to remain calm and plan on how to get away. If he leaves any opening, bolt and run. If you are prone and he tries to rape you, as he gets close, quickly place a foot on his chest, shoving as hard as you can. This will only gain you a few seconds time, but may be enough time to escape from a room. It may allow you to stand up and then defend yourself with knee kicks and palm strikes. If he is on top of you, get him to relax his guard by sweet talking to him so you can get your hands free. Once your hands are free, wrap one arm around his head and bring it in close to you. Take your other hand and stick your thumb as deeply into his eye as your can. It is very painful and he will immediately jerk back. This is why you have your arm around his head, hold on, and continue drilling your thumb deeply into his eye. He will fight to get away because of the pain. As soon as you let go, make your escape. This eye gouge is not pleasant and might cause injury to his eye, but you may be saving your life.

- Leave as much physical evidence around as you can such as hair, fibers, scraps of cloth and blood for future prosecution.

- If a group of men are intent on assaulting you, it is an extremely difficult situation. The best approach is to try to determine the leader and get him to take you somewhere that the two of you can be alone. This allows you try to deal with one person instead of a group. You have a much better chance of escape. You may be able to talk and reason with him, get him to change his mind, gain his sympathy or get him to let you go. If it is unavoidable, you must survive. As difficult as it may be, try to relax your body to minimize internal damage.

- If you are raped, go to a friend's house or where you can get emotional support. Get medical help at the local hospital immediately. Tell them what happened. They have rape evidence kits. Do not shower or do anything to destroy any potential evidence. Do take a change of clothes since your clothes will probably be held as evidence. Do talk with the police and ask for a female officer. Law enforcement now handles rape cases with much more sensitivity than in the past. Talking with the police does not mean you have to press charges, but I encourage you to do so, since the criminal will likely continue his behavior unless stopped. You may save some other woman and she would be eternally grateful to you. Contact a local rape crisis counseling center or contact RAINN at 1-800-656-HOPE.

National Sex Offender Public Registry

The U.S. Department of Justice has a National Sex Offender Public Registry at www.nsopr.gov which links to state databases detailing the known location of sexual offenders. You can search by name, state, city or zip code. It will give you a description of the offender, their photograph, address, crime committed, and status. You can use the site to map their address to see how close they may be to your location or residence.

Let's review **Rape and Sexual Assault Prevention**:

✓ An acquaintance is more likely to be an assailant than a stranger.
✓ College freshman are the most at risk for date rape.
✓ Drink very moderately or not at all.

- ✓ Don't allow yourself to be isolated.
- ✓ Beware of date rape drugs.
- ✓ Communicate your expectations.
- ✓ Stop the momentum if things start progressing too fast.
- ✓ Make a quick decision when faced with sexual assault.
- ✓ Act on whatever that decision is quickly and fully.
- ✓ Get help if you have been sexually assaulted and report the crime.

Chapter 6

Stalking

Stalking is continued unwanted contact, whether direct or indirect, from an individual that intimidates and causes the object of their attention to fear for their safety. It may occur by being followed, watched, receiving unwanted letters or emails, unwanted telephone calls and other harassing actions. The ways stalkers harass their victims is only limited by their imagination. Since 1995, there are laws against stalking in every state.

Stalkers are divided into three types:

- Partner – This can be an ex-spouse, ex-intimate partner or someone else you no longer date. They don't want to give up that relationship, and believe if they just persist they can get it back.

- Delusional – This person fantasizes the person will be or is interested in them. They may believe they have a relationship with that person even when they may have never met them. Movie stars are good examples of the targets of this type of stalker, but they may also be a teacher, doctor, minister, married woman or other person.

- Angry – Some issue has upset the stalker and he is seeking to intimidate or harm the person he believes influenced or controls that issue. Politicians are frequent victims of this type of stalker.

Stalkers can be dangerous, so do not take any stalking threat lightly. John Lennon was stalked and killed by Mark David Chapman in 1980. There are many other examples. Ex-spouses, in particular, may not want to give up the relationship and may cause harm to the victim in retaliation or "if I can't have the relationship then nobody will."

Some statistics on stalking:

- One million women are stalked annually.
- Average stalking lasts 1.8 years.
- 78% of all stalking victims are women.
- 77% of those women know their stalkers.
- 43% report the stalking started after a relationship ended.
- 48% of stalkers were spouses, ex-spouses or intimate partners and 81% of these stalkers physically assaulted their victims.

Source: Stalking in America – Findings From the National Violence Against Women Survey, Tjaden, Patricia, Thoennes, Nancy 1998

What To Do

- Tell the individual, you believe to be a stalker, "NO." Do this only once since repeating this is giving continual attention to the stalker.
- Contact an anti-stalking organization or other woman's help group for support and assistance. You can contact AWARE at 1-877-67-AWARE. Use the internet to access the National Center for Victims of Crime, www.ncvc.org. This site has the stalking laws for each state. If you do not have a computer at home, go to the nearest library.
- Talk with police and the local prosecutor.
- Document all instances of harassment. Save letters and emails as evidence. Take photos of any injuries, damage and any time the stalker is out in front of the home. Use a camera that notes the date on the picture.
- Be very careful of stalkers who are spouses, ex-spouses and ex-intimate partners because these stalkers are more likely to physically assault their victims. Take every precaution to keep them at a distance and be on high alert if they get near.
- Change all of your locks immediately.
- Change your email and answering machine passwords to prevent remote accessing of your messages.
- Have the lock on your mailbox changed or if it can't be locked

you may want to rent a post office box for a period of time.

- Get a new unlisted telephone number and give it only to your friends. Keep your old number active with an answering machine so the stalker can call that number. If you terminate the old number, the stalker will just try to find the new telephone number or some other way to harass you.

- Tell family, friends and neighbors what is going on.

- Try to vary your times and routes.

- If you suspect you are being followed, turn a number of corners and if the car is still there, go to the nearest police station. Do not go home or to a friend's home.

- Make sure your gas tank has a locking cap either from the inside of the car or is the type that requires a key to unlock the cap. This prevents someone putting contaminants in the gas tank. Keep your car in a locked garage whenever possible.

- Advise your employer about what is going on. Arrange to have your co-workers screen your calls and any visitors. Have your name removed from any parking spot.

- Go to Google on the internet and have your name blocked so your telephone and address will not be given out. Have your name blocked at the Department of Motor Vehicles and Voter Registration.

- Consider getting a dog. Dogs are great crime deterrents.

- Consider obtaining a restraining order because police can use the order to take action if it is violated. Be prepared for it to be violated, since statistics indicate it will be violated 69% of the time. While a restraining order in many cases can help, it can also cause some stalkers to up the ante to perhaps violence since they may feel humiliated or thwarted in their actions.

- Consider having the police talk to the stalker to advise him that any actions violating the law, including stalking, will be not be tolerated and will be prosecuted to the full extent of the law. Sometimes this "counseling" will cause the stalker to cease.

- Review all of the preventative measures under the **Avoidance** section.

- Consider moving.

- Take a woman's self-defense class and consider enrolling in a martial arts school. See Self-Defense Training and Martial Arts in Chapter 12.

The three ways stalking most often cease are; the victim moves, the police talk with the stalker, and the stalker finds a new love interest. Unfortunately, you normally can't accelerate the last one.

I encourage you to report any stalking to the police. Stalking is a serious crime and the sooner the police are aware of the problem, the sooner they can be a factor in getting the stalking to stop.

College Women

College women experience a higher level of stalking than the average population, although it normally lasts a shorter period of time. The primary perpetrators are boyfriends, ex-boyfriends and classmates. The methods of stalking used most often were telephoning, waiting, watching, following the victim, and sending letters and emails.

Statistics
- 13% of college women are stalked.
- Average length of time is two months.
- 15% were threatened or some attempt was made to harm them.
- 17% of the time the stalking was reported to police.
- 93% told someone, usually a friend, that they were being stalked.
- 66% were boyfriends, ex-boyfriends or classmates.

Source: Fisher, Bonnie S., Cullen, Francis T., Turner, Michael G. Sexual Victimization of College Women, US Department of Justice, Nation Institute of Justice 2000

The main reasons for the low reporting rate to the police were the women didn't consider it serious enough, didn't realize it was against the law and felt the police wouldn't take action.

Just to reiterate, stalking is serious every time because you don't know what the stalker's true intentions are, and it could turn ugly or violent. I urge you to be very careful if you are being stalked and contact police along with appropriate college officials.

Let's review **Stalking**:

- ✓ Stalking is a serious problem.
- ✓ Contact an anti-stalking organization for help.
- ✓ Tell police and document all harassment.
- ✓ Consider legal action.
- ✓ Have police talk to stalker.

Chapter 7

Domestic Violence

Domestic violence is unfortunately all too common. It occurs in cities, small towns and rural areas. It is in rich families and poor families. It is all about achieving power and control over the other partner by using fear and intimidation. One spouse, typically the male, uses verbal and physical intimidation to exert control over his partner. The abuse may start slowly, but over time can escalate from verbal abuse to shoving, to hitting, to severe beatings. He wants to dominate the relationship. He may isolate her by denying access to credit cards or checking accounts, and not letting her visit friends or family. She may suffer from low self esteem after being verbally abused with, "You're ugly, stupid, worthless, etc." Many times the woman rationalizes that it is really her fault and if she only corrects certain things everything will be fine. He reinforces this thinking with comments like, "It's your fault. You made me hit you." Nothing could be further from the truth! No woman is going to make a man hit her. She may feel that she loves the man and she can somehow get him to correct his behavior. The man, between incidents, may behave in an exemplary manner reinforcing the woman's feeling that she is making progress, only to be abused once again, perhaps even more violently. It is like being on a roller coaster. She typically hides the signs of the abuse not wanting anyone to know there is a problem.

The man may be perceived by the community as a nice guy because he keeps his abusive side so well hidden. The woman may feel trapped because of children, limited financial options, threats of further violence including possible homicide, embarrassment, social status, concerns about becoming a single parent, feelings of responsibility to make the marriage work, feeling divorce is not an option, no perceived place to go, and she may believe she still loves the man.

If your partner controls your every move, verbally abuses you, intimidates you, forces you to have sex when you don't want to, or hits you in any manner, you are a victim of domestic violence. Admit to yourself that there is a problem and that something has to be done. This may be the hardest part.

Action Plan

- Contact a local domestic violence center. If there is no local center call the National Domestic Violence Hotline, 1-800-799-SAFE, for help and advice.
- Tell trusted friends, family and your minister what is going on. Establish a code word so that they know when to call for help.
- Document all abuse noting times and dates. Have pictures taken of any physical injuries.
- Talk to a legal advisor about your options.
- Your computer activities and email may be read by your partner or spouse. *Do not* use your computer or your home email account to communicate about any concerns or where you might go. Use the computers at libraries and outside telephones so the phone logs can not be tracked. Set up a hotmail.com or gmail.com email account, which are free, that only you can access. Go to the library to access your new account and send email. You can use your home computer to lay a false trail, if necessary, by searching for hotels or seeking information about a location where you don't intend to go.
- If an argument starts, go to a room in the house that doesn't have any weapons like knives or guns. Keep guns unloaded and locked up if you can.
- Try to identify trigger points and if you see them coming, go to a neighbor's or other safe location.
- Talk to your children about what is going on. Tell the children not to interfere or get involved when you and your spouse are arguing or there is violence. Keep your children safe by keeping them out of the arguments. Make sure they know how to dial 911 in an emergency. Arrange a code word with your children to let them know if they should go to a neighbor's home.

- If you are being beaten, utilize the self-defense techniques detailed in chapter 4, or if you are unable to defend yourself, curl into a ball in a corner and protect your head.

- If the police come, tell them what is going on. Do not tell them everything is fine.

- Begin to think about what needs to be done if you have to leave. Make copies of all important documents such as deeds, insurance, social security card, driver's license, credit cards, W-2's, tax records, passport, medical cards, prescriptions, and bank accounts. Keep this information with a trusted friend or family member.

- Find ways to save some cash to use if you have to leave. Keep this with a trusted friend or family member.

- Take some clothes for you and your children over to a trusted friend's house in case you have to leave.

- Develop plausible excuses why you need to leave the home at various times, such as going to grocery store, returning a book to the library, taking out the garbage, returning a movie, etc.

- Plan on how to get out of the house and if you have to leave, just walk out, perhaps using one of your reasons for leaving. Other times you may just want to go out the door and keep going. Go quickly to your preplanned destination.

- Always keep your gas tank at least half full and back your car into the driveway so you can leave immediately if necessary.

- Make a spare key for the car in case your spouse takes your keys.

- Keep change with you allowing you to make a telephone call if your cell phone is taken from you.

- If you have particularly special or sentimental items, like pictures or a vase, take them to a trusted friend. If you leave, there is a high probability your spouse will destroy those items in retaliation or a fit of anger.

- Consider getting a protective order. This will give you a legal basis to ask police and others to take action. Be prepared for it to be violated.

- Notify your family, friends, neighbors, and your employer that you have left the relationship.

- Notify the children's school and use the protective order to insure the school understands that your spouse is not authorized to pick up your children without your approval.

- If he leaves, *change the locks*. Change the password on your telephone answering machine and your email account so he can not access either one remotely. Meet him in a public place with lots of people around when you must meet for discussions, or for him to pick up the children for the weekend.

- Varying your routine and routes makes it is less likely it can be anticipated where you will be at a given time.

- Before you leave, you may want to lay a false trail. You can leave information that will be found indicating you are somewhere, different state etc., other than where you intend to be. Telephone a motel in a different state (he may check the phone log), or leave pamphlets, maps or other material leading in the wrong direction.

- If you leave, tell only very trusted individuals where you are.

If you think you may be in a domestic violence situation, I strongly encourage you to contact your local domestic violence center.

Let's review **Domestic Violence**:

- ✓ If you are a victim of domestic violence develop an action plan. Do not ignore violence or believe it will get better.
- ✓ Get legal advice.
- ✓ Tell close friends and family what's going on.
- ✓ Prepare a plan to possibly leave and stash things at a friend's.
- ✓ Leave if necessary.
- ✓ Get help and advice from a local domestic crisis center.

Chapter 8

Children

W hile this book is primarily designed as a guide for the basic safety of women, women also feel a strong responsibility to protect the family. A woman may disregard her own safety concerns, but she will become a lioness if any of her children are threatened. We will discuss ways to enhance the safety of children. Children are special responsibilities and require our best efforts. Let me begin with a few rules that you need to abide by:

★ *Be a good role model.* They learn more from you than anywhere else.
★ *No substance abuse that will affect you or the children.*
★ *No abuse of the children.* If the situation is too much for you, seek help from a friend or other resource where you can get assistance.

I have divided the safety ideas for children into five general age groups. For all age groups, be informed, review the information regarding accessing the National Sex Offender Public registry on page 109.

Daycare

■ Check multiple references regarding the daycare facility and personnel. Talk with other parents about their experiences with the daycare.

■ Ask how they screen their employees and what precautions they take to ensure these employees are suitable for being around young children.

- Make several visits at different times to observe how the facility is being operated prior to enrolling your child.
- Make sure you can visit the facility at *any* time in the future.
- Verify there are two adults in attendance at the facility at all times.
- Verify that only an authorized adult can pick up a child. Understand what is required for a valid authorization.
- Ask how they handle behavior problems.
- Ask what their policy is on sick children and how they handle those that become sick while at the facility.
- Be very suspicious of changes in your child's behavior.

Preschool Age

- Make sure they know your first and last name, address and telephone number. Rehearse this with them.
- Teach children that uniformed police and firemen are their friends.
- Play the "what if" game with them to develop answers for various situations. As an example, ask the child what they would do if they ever get separated from you in a store or crowd. Agree on an appropriate answer.
- Teach the child how to dial 911 as soon as they are old enough to be able to do this responsibly.
- Have your child fingerprinted and obtain a DNA kit or preserve fingernail and hair clippings. Make sure you have a current picture. DNA kits are available from several companies that you can find on the internet.
- All children must be properly restrained in car seats while riding in vehicles. You can check the different state law requirements at the Insurance Institute for Highway Safety: www.iihs.org /laws/state_laws/restrain2.html.
- Never leave your child alone in the car or yard for even just an instant. Tragedy can happen fast. There was a recent incident in St. Louis where a woman left her car running while she went into a store for a quick errand. Upon returning she found her car had been stolen with her child in it.

- You should check the National Sex Offender Registry at the U.S. Department of Justice, http://www.nsopr.gov, to determine if there are any offenders living nearby. Be aware that not all sex offenders register and the information may not be current.

- Minimize a stranger's opportunity to access your child by assuring they are always accompanied by or in the care of a trusted adult.

- Begin to teach them about stranger danger and that no one should touch their private parts but their parents, a doctor or nurse. It is not only about strangers because relatives and friends can also victimize children.

- Mark your children's belongings with only their initials like ABC. If you have their name on them, someone could call to the child.

- Check babysitter references and get to know the family. Leave emergency contact numbers with the babysitter. Make sure the babysitter understands that no one is allowed in the home while you are gone.

- Make sure all poisons and medications are locked up. Make sure children cannot get to household chemicals such as; drain cleaner, dishwasher detergent, bleach, oven cleaner, etc. - the list is long.

- If you own firearms, keep them and all ammunition locked up.

- Teach your child to leave any firearm alone. If they find one, leave it and report it to a parent.

School Age

- Update fingerprints, DNA samples, and pictures.

- *Listen to your children carefully.* Respond to any of their concerns. The child should be told secrets can be dangerous and they should not keep secrets from you.

- Update and play the "what if" game with them. Go through various "what if" scenarios with your child to help them anticipate potential problems and what they should do about them.

- Explain to the child that good strangers always leave children alone.

- Teach the child that uniformed police officers and firemen are their friends.
- Teach the child to run to where other people are if a stranger bothers them. They should immediately tell you, a teacher, police officer or other trusted adult.
- Teach the child to run if a stranger tries to entice them with candy, toy or asks them to help search for a puppy. They should run if a stranger asks for assistance. They should say "NO" and GO. They should immediately tell you, a teacher, police officer or other trusted adult about any incident.
- Tell the child when going to a public restroom to go with a trusted adult or to use the buddy system.
- Teach the child what to do if they get separated in a crowd or while shopping. Make sure the child knows your cell phone number.
- If the child is feeling uncomfortable or threatened, they should go to a woman or trusted public official (policeman/fireman).
- Tell children never to go anywhere with a stranger, such as getting in his car or going into his home. If a stranger comes up saying a parent has been hurt and the child is to go with them or a similar message, the child should immediately run to the nearest place of safety such as a school, home or neighbor's. They should quickly tell a trusted adult about the incident.
- Agree on a code word with the child, to indicate the stranger is a friend, like "purple ice cream" or other non-typical words. A boy was recently lost on a Boy Scout trip and while he saw the searchers looking for him, he did what he had been taught to do, which was stay away from strangers. So he stayed hidden. Fortunately he was eventually found. If you have a code word, the searchers can say, "John, purple ice cream."
- Teach the child that if a playmate gets into a car with a stranger, they should try to write down the license plate number, even in the dirt or on the sidewalk with a rock, and report it to the nearest trusted adult.
- Tell them never to open a door to a stranger and never ever let them in the house.
- Tell them never to let a stranger or a friend touch them on their

private parts. No one except their parents, a doctor or nurse should touch their private parts defined as whatever is covered by their bathing suit. It is a fact that a lot of relatives and acquaintances have been involved in child abuse so it is not just strangers that the child has to watch out for.

- Teach them how to answer the phone appropriately and never let anyone know they are home alone. Let the answering machine answer so the child can "vet" the call prior to answering.
- Do not allow them to go to the playground or movies alone. Use the buddy system.
- Do not allow them to go out after dark alone.
- Tell them that it is okay to tell you or a trusted adult if someone hurt them or made them scared.
- Teach them to walk on the side facing traffic. It is safer since they can see the oncoming traffic and no one can coast up behind to grab them and put them in a car.
- Walk to school or to the bus stop the first few days to reassure them and make sure there are no problems. If there are problems, consider the walk *your* daily exercise routine.
- Get to know the bus driver by their first name. At the end of the day ask the child about school and include the bus ride.
- Place children in bedrooms that do not have easy access to the outside.
- Keep bedroom doors open so that you can hear if there are any problems.
- Make sure fire alarms are working and practice a fire drill to get out of the house. Agree on a prearranged spot to meet after escape from the house.
- Teach your child to keep doors and windows locked.
- Teach your child some basic self-defense techniques, especially how to escape grasps. Consider enrolling the child in a martial arts class.
- Teach them to give up their coat or other possession if a stranger grabs it. If their coat is grabbed, they should relax their arms; let their arms go behind them sliding out of the coat, and run.
- Visit the school and verify appropriate security precautions are in place.

- On field trips there should be a minimum of one parent on each bus, communication between buses or vehicles, a roll call each time a bus/vehicle is loaded, and if possible, a matching brightly colored t-shirt to help with identification. Each student should have a card with the name of the school and telephone number in case they get separated from the group.
- Check to see who is allowed to pick up students after school and what authorization is required.
- Tell child not to discuss the family's financial status or what material things they might have indicating wealth or different social status.
- Encourage the children to make a number of friends.
- Do not just drop off the child at a friend's house the first time. Go in, introduce yourself and ascertain everything is appropriate. You may wish to ask if there are firearms in the home and if so, are they secured such that children cannot get to them. Have the child call you for permission any time there are plans to go to another location.
- Do not allow the child to go to school with more than a small amount of money and no valuables.
- Tell the child that if they are physically threatened, they should give up the money or other possession, and report the loss immediately to a teacher or other trusted adult.
- Tell the child that if they are being bullied to report that to school authorities and to you. Sixty percent of bullying is done by boys and 40% is committed by girls. Bullying is most prevalent in grades 7 to 9 and next in grades 4 to 6. Tell the child not to participate in bullying.

Teenage

- Update fingerprints, DNA samples, and pictures.
- Make sure your teenagers, particularly daughters, have cell phones. I consider this extremely important. It allows them to call you anytime they have a problem or need help. Make sure the cell phone you get comes with a global positioning system or GPS, that allows the cell phone to be located if 911 is called. The

telephone service provider can locate the phone via the GPS if requested by law enforcement. There are software programs that allow you to track the phone from your home computer in real time. For a monthly fee you can know the location and speed the phone (car) is going. This will tell you exactly where your teen is at as long as the phone is turned on.

- Make sure they understand they can call you anytime, anyplace and you will come and get them *without asking any questions.* Make this agreement with your child and keep it. She will talk about the problem if she wants to, but in the meantime you will help her preserve her dignity and more importantly, remove her from a dangerous or deteriorating situation. She is more likely to call you if she knows she is not going to get the 3rd degree or face an inquisition.
- Listen to your child carefully and be supportive of issues she may have. Always keep the lines of communication open, possibly preventing more serious problems from developing.
- Talk to them about dressing and acting appropriately.
- Discuss sex and rape with your daughter.
- Teach them that it is perfectly fine to say, "No! I don't want to do that."
- Teach them it is okay not to go along with the crowd. In fact, they will be more respected for being their own person.
- Tell them it is alright to use you as an excuse. "My parents would kill me/disown me if I did that." Then you must back them up with friends, if necessary, saying something like, "No! That is unacceptable."
- Know where they are going, with whom and what time they should return. Girls, when your parents ask these questions it is because they love you and want you to be safe. You shouldn't take offense that they ask questions about where you are planning to go; instead you should volunteer this information.
- Before accepting any part time job they need to talk with you. Make sure it is a legitimate job for a reputable person/firm. Understand what their duties are and what is expected of them. Under no circumstances should they go into a customer's house if they have a job requiring going door to door, such as a paper route.

- Before your daughter accepts a babysitting job, you should check out the family and make sure there is a list of emergency numbers in case of a problem while the parents are gone.

- Traveling in a group is better than going alone. Two is better than one and three is better than two, etc.

- It is unacceptable to entertain any male guest alone (or be entertained in his home) without a parent at home.

- Before your daughter stays overnight with a friend, get to know the parents. Before she goes over to spend the night, verify with the parents they plan to be there and are aware of the plans.

- An aisle seat is better at the movies than a seat in the middle of the row since you can move if there is a problem.

- Teach them running away is a better option than getting into a car even if a weapon is displayed. See appropriate section in Chapter 4 - **Action.**

- Teach/learn some self-defense techniques. Consider enrollment in a martial arts class. Attend personal safety classes. Like all things, some are better than others, but you will pick up some ideas on how to reduce your risk of becoming a victim.

- Establish code words or phrases indicating there is a problem, thereby alerting you to a problem without causing them to lose face with their friends. Examples might be; "Is the cat or dog still sick?" or "How are Aunt Sue or Uncle Joe feeling?" Pick your own phrase that is easy to remember and relevant to the family.

- The computer should be in a common area where activities can be viewed by everyone. Computer activities should be monitored! Nothing should be sent on email or posted to chat rooms that couldn't be put on the kitchen bulletin board. Learn how to check which URL sites have been visited. (In Internet Explorer - click on View in the upper left hand toolbar. When the View box opens, click on Explorer Bar, and then click on the history option. Netscape, Safari and Firefox have ways to view history as well.) This is not being disrespectful of their privacy; rather this is being done to help protect your child. All large companies have polices regarding the fact that employee emails will be monitored and your family policy should be the same. Teach them to never give out personal information, never upload their picture to someone they don't know, don't respond to any suggestive postings and never, never agree to meet someone they met online. The U.S. Department of Justice's publication: *Highlights of the Youth Internet Safety Survey*, March 2001 estimates that 19% of youths 10 to 17 years old receive unwanted sexual solicitations online. It is probably much higher today. **I highly recommend that you visit the FBI's website and look at the FBI publication:** *A Parent's Guide to Internet Safety* **at www.fbi.gov/publications.** Other suggested information can be found at www.cybertipline.com, www.netsmartz.com, www.safeteens.com, www.wiredsafety.org, and www.microsoft.com/athome/security/children.

- Teach them to stay away from isolated spots and never allow themselves to be isolated.

- Teach them never go to the beach or a park after dark or if they do, only with a large group and STAY with the group.

- Teach them that alcohol makes boys much more aggressive and can adversely affect normally good judgment – both theirs and their companions.

- Be a good role model. If you drink, do so only in moderation, never to the point of intoxication. Don't do drugs period. Encourage them not to drink, get drunk or do drugs. These all negatively affect their lives and their personal safety.

- Do not condone underage drinking.

- *NEVER EVER* provide alcohol for your child's underage friends for parties under the guise of "they will get it anyway and I would rather be here" or to be "a friend" to your child. *It is illegal!* You can be charged with a crime, and if there are other problems, you may be subject to civil penalties. As an example, if anyone leaves and has an accident, you may be liable. It is totally irresponsible on your part and violates your commitment to being a good role model. Your child will actually think less of you since they know it is illegal and wrong. Your child thinks you are a hero and can walk on water – don't blow it. Keep high standards because they learn from you.

- Be involved with your children and attend their school events and after school activities such as drama, musical endeavors or athletic competitions. Be positive, but not demanding about their activities.

- Beware if they have a marked change in personality, sleeping habits, and/or appearance; school grades suddenly becoming much lower, along with good friends being replaced by questionable friends; they no longer seem to be interested in hobbies or activities that really interested them in the past. You should investigate the reason for the change in habits to determine if there is drug involvement or some other traumatic or emotional event.

- Tell them not to ride with anyone who is under the influence. There are too many incidents of an innocent person being injured by a driver that was under the influence. They need to get out and make that call to you to come and get them. Remember, no questions asked. It may take a little courage but it may be *their* life that *they* are saving.

- Teens report that 13% of them have been physically abused by their boyfriends and 26% say they have suffered verbal abuse. Girls - ***Do not stay in an abusive relationship!*** Abuse doesn't get better, it only gets worse. Don't think for a minute that you will be able to change the guy. He may promise he will never do it again, but that lasts only until the next time he gets mad. The solution to abuse is to leave the relationship and date someone else who respects you. There are lots of cute boys out there who are not abusive and respect women. Do not tolerate abuse.

- As a teenager, if you are part of a family where sexual abuse, assault or violence occurs, you should talk with a trusted adult. This could be a relative, teacher, religious leader, or the parent of a good friend. I know this will be difficult, but you have to get help to deal with this very destructive and dangerous situation.

College Age

- A room on the 2nd floor is better than the first floor. The windows are much harder to get at. The 3rd floor is better than second. Being above the 7th floor increases your risk in case of a fire since many fire truck ladders will not reach above this level.

- Have a way to secure your valuables such as a drawer or file cabinet that can be locked.

- Always lock your doors and windows. Lock your door even it you are just going down the hall.
- Always close curtains and blinds.
- Get to know your roommates/friends before fully trusting them.
- Keep doors locked to the building and don't give out the door combinations or let in strangers.
- Do your laundry with someone else during the daytime. Laundry rooms are typically in remote areas of the building.
- Try not to walk alone at night. Walking with a group is much better.
- Avoid deserted areas at night.
- If you are studying in the library, try to stay in a room with more than four people.
- Use bathrooms that have a lock on the inside.
- Most colleges provide an escort service at night. Take advantage of it and other campus security measures.
- Tell your roommates where you are going, with whom and the time you should return.
- Avoid/minimize alcohol consumption.
- College can be very busy and stressful. Don't overbook yourself with too many activities reducing your normal level of alertness.
- Always carry your cell phone and keep it charged.
- If you are going out, take your driver's license, a credit card and some cash. Leave your purse at home and you won't have to keep track of it in a crowded place or while you are out on the dance floor.
- Pay your own way. If someone wants to buy you one drink fine, but not more than that. You don't want to set up any expectations.
- Stay with a group of friends when you are at parties.
- Agree ahead of time with your friend(s) that you will watch out for each other and will get help for the person that exhibits loss of control due to alcohol or drugs. You will not allow them to leave with anyone in this condition and definitely not with a stranger. Friends watching out for each other can be one of the

best things to prevent potential pain and heartache.

- Stay in rooms with mixed genders and avoid any room that only has guys drinking.
- Do not give out personal information or your address. Give your email for a contact number if you want to since you can block that or change email addresses if necessary.
- Do not accept rides from strangers or anyone you don't know really well.
- Do not leave a party or bar with a stranger or someone you don't know really well.
- Be especially wary of college athletic and fraternity parties that have alcohol. College athletes, in particular, can get a misguided sense of themselves and feel an entitlement when comes to women.
- *The section on date rape prevention should be mandatory reading for any young women entering college.*

Missing

If a child is missing it is imperative to start looking as soon as possible with all of the appropriate resources that can be mustered. The sooner the search starts, the higher the probability of finding the child alive.

- Provide the police with a complete description of the child, what he was wearing, where last seen and provide a photo. Always keep two photos in your purse, one to give police and one to be able to show.
- Cooperate with police and understand that you will be a suspect. Get cleared as quickly as possible and establish trust with the police. Let the police do their job.
- Contact the National Center for Missing and Exploited Children at 1-800-THE-LOST.
- Call local media providing them with photos and descriptive information. Establish a partnership with them to keep the search in the news.
- Have someone monitor your telephone 24/7.
- Organize a search with family, friends, neighbors, co-workers

and any volunteers that you can get.
- Get flyers and posters to publicize the search.
- Consider a reward.

Molested

If your child has been molested it can be devastating for the child and you. The child is the most important part of this equation and needs all of the care and support that can be given.

- Stay calm no matter how outraged you are. Your child needs support and it will not help if you go to pieces.
- Be reassuring to your child. Be very supportive and express your continuing love for them.
- If the child has suffered injury, get him or her to a doctor or emergency room. Explain what has happened to the medical personnel so they understand what they are dealing with.
- Call the police. They have experts in dealing with these issues.
- Obtain therapy for the child.

Let's review **Children**:

- ✓ Be a good role model.
- ✓ Have children fingerprinted, continually update photographs and get a DNA kit.
- ✓ Communicate with your child regarding his/her safety and what he/she should do.
- ✓ Listen to them carefully.
- ✓ Have them travel in groups or use the buddy system whenever possible.
- ✓ It is OK for them not to "go along" with their group.
- ✓ You will come get them at any time with no questions asked.
- ✓ Never ever provide alcohol for anyone that is underage.
- ✓ Have them read the chapter on date rape prevention at the appropriate age.
- ✓ Get immediate help if the child is missing or has been molested.

Chapter 9

Elderly

The elderly are especially vulnerable to abuse and crime because of advancing age they are neither as physically or mentally capable of defending themselves as when they were younger. The most common types of crimes against seniors are:

- Financial crimes
- Property crimes
- Violent crimes
- Elderly abuse

Seniors have been used to making all of their own financial decisions before, but now may not recognize the risk of the new "cyber" crime or possibly their own diminished mental agility. They are vulnerable to financial crime since many of them are very polite and don't wish to offend someone by interrupting or hanging up.

Preventing Financial Crime

- Follow all of the suggestions in Chapter 11, the section on **Identity Theft**.

- Before a senior makes a financial decision, have him or her consult with someone that is trusted. That could be one of their children, a financial advisor or trusted friend. This will help prevent scams or purchasing unneeded services. The senior can then always say, "Sorry, I have to talk with my advisor about that." eliminating the requirement for him or her to make a quick decision. This is particularly true if there is a request to sign any legal documents.

- If a deal sounds too good to be true, it probably is. Seniors should always pass when the seller is pressuring them and insisting on immediate purchase.
- Seniors should not participate in telephone surveys and not buy anything over the phone unless they initiated the call.
- Ask for details of any offer to be sent by U.S. Mail and save the envelope. If there is a problem later it allows the U.S. Postal Inspector to get involved.
- Have Social Security and other routine checks direct deposited.
- You should consider giving power of attorney to a *trustworthy* family member and have them as a co-signer on your bank account. If there is a sudden change in health or other adverse issue, they would be able step in and help take care of your affairs immediately. Note that I highlighted *trustworthy* because I am aware of several situations where family members have abused this privilege. You may wish to discuss this issue with your attorney and make any decision carefully.
- Make sure all financial assets (credit reports, checking accounts, investment accounts, etc.) are routinely monitored to make sure there are no problems.

Property Crime

The elderly are more prone than any other age group to property crime. Follow all of the suggestions in the chapters on **Awareness** and **Avoidance**.

Violent Crime

Seniors have the lowest rate of violent crime in comparison to their proportion of the population. As noted previously, follow all of the suggestions in the chapters on **Attitude, Awareness** and **Avoidance**. I want to emphasize that going with one or more friends, as noted in the prior chapters, is particularly good for seniors.

Elderly Abuse

Because of diminished physical and mental capacity, the elderly are often abused, neglected or financially exploited. They need to be monitored regularly by a trustworthy person, whether the elderly person lives in their own home or some type of assisted living facility. The need for checking and assistance will depend greatly on their physical and mental capabilities. Each set of circumstances will be unique to that individual or couple. There is no way to ascertain their ongoing welfare without routine visits. I suggest this be divided between several family members or designated professionals. Checks should be made on the living facilities, the physical and metal health of the individual, and verify finances are in order.

Financial Red Flags

- Sudden large change (loss) in the value of their assets that cannot be explained.
- Assets suddenly being transferred to someone, accounts becoming joint or new signatories being added.
- Sudden changes to their will.
- Sudden large withdrawals from the bank or investment accounts.
- Large checks written to cash.
- Large credit card charges for items they don't have or wouldn't typically buy.
- Jewelry or other valuable items suddenly missing.

Home

- Make sure you arrange for routine visits by family, friends, or someone hired to check periodically. Communicate regularly by telephone and email.
- Consider a security system with a panic button lavaliere that they can wear as appropriate.
- Check the house to determine if locks are working on doors and windows. Check to see if outside security lights are working. Consider putting dusk to dawn lights or motion detector lights at the back door or in the back yard. Consider installing a motion detector light at the front and back doors.
- Check their driving skills to make sure they are still safe to have a license.

- Check all medications and verify usage. Check for contraindications to make sure there are no drug interaction problems with other medications or foods.
- Eliminate unsecured floor coverings and eliminate clutter that poses a tripping hazard.
- Make sure there is a working fire alarm. Check to make sure power cords are not frayed; not tripping hazards and are not overloading the electrical circuits.
- A cane can be a very effective weapon. Teach them how to use it. It should be used in a jabbing motion, like a pool cue, targeting the throat, face and solar plexus.

Assisted Living

- The good news is abuse and problems in nursing homes have declined dramatically with the rigid reporting now required. Every nursing home is required to make available a copy of the survey of its facilities noting any problems or citations. It will be three to six months behind, but you will get an idea if there are problems.
- Check the ranking of the facility within the state. This can be done by contacting the appropriate state health care agency.
- Check lots of references.
- Check the cleanliness and appearance of employees. You should do a smell test of the facility. It should not smell of urine or spoiled food. If things are sloppy, find another place.
- Do not let the elderly person have any valuables such as rings, jewelry or cash with them, these will disappear.
- Consider installing a camera tied into the internet that allows you to monitor the room at any time.
- If a family member is the primary caregiver, routine checks should still be made. More abuse now occurs in home settings than in nursing homes. Are there unexplained bruises? Does the elderly person seem fearful or hesitant to talk about bruises? Many elderly people will disguise their abuse because they are unwilling to betray family members and are afraid of the alternative.

- Share the responsibilities of care giving since this will give the primary caregiver a break and allow you to assess any potential problems up close.
- The elderly person should have a "living will" to advise others of their wishes. This will save the family much anguish if a decision has to be made regarding continued use of life support machines or other heroic medical measures.

An excellent resource is the National Center on Elder Abuse which can be accessed at www.elderabusecenter.org.

Let's review **Elderly**:

- ✓ Arrange for a trusted advisor for the senior.
- ✓ Make sure there are routine visits.
- ✓ Check for any safety issues in their living facilities.
- ✓ Investigate carefully before making a decision on assisted living.
- ✓ Discuss having a living will with them.

Chapter 10

Travel

Before you leave for that business trip or long delayed dream vacation, there are some things you need to do to protect your property.

Before you leave

- Cancel the newspaper and put your mail on hold.
- Arrange to have your lawn mowed.
- Put lights, radios and TV's on timers.
- Place any valuables or important documents in your bank safety deposit box.
- Make two color copies of your passport & visas, one to take with you and one to leave with a friend.
- Carry the minimum number of credit cards.
- Use the type of holder that goes around the neck or waist and under clothing for money & passport.
- Split cash & cards among travelers.
- Leave your answering machine on.
- Lock your garage door and disengage the opener.
- Have neighbors routinely check your home.
- Have your neighbor park his car in your driveway.
- Give your itinerary, a set of house and car keys to family or to a trusted neighbor or friend.
- Consider having a house sitter while you are gone. Do a background check on the sitter.

- Minimize the amount of luggage you take.
- Make list of serial numbers of electronic equipment you're taking with you.
- Take spare medications, contacts and/or glasses.
- Don't tell casual acquaintances you will be gone.

Avoid packing anything in luggage that you don't want to lose. Try to put any items of value in your carry-on bags where you keep them with you and secure.

Airports

- Schedule direct flights whenever possible.
- Put your business address and telephone number on your luggage tags.
- Do not place any valuables in your checked luggage. It wasn't safe before, and now that you have to check unlocked luggage it is even less.
- In order to lock your checked luggage, buy TSA recognized locking mechanisms. These "special" locks can be opened by the TSA using tools provided by the lock manufacturers. Travel Sentry and Safe Skies make locks that are TSA "friendly." Check the TSA web site at www.tsa.gov for more information.
- Place your toiletries, a change of clothes and any medications in your carry-on bag. If your bags are delayed, you can still operate. Note: security regulations change frequently so understand the latest rules concerning carry-on before you travel.
- Pack toothbrushes and other personal items in plastic bags so security personnel aren't directly touching them when they go through your bags.
- Use electrical ties, the plastic strips used for tying electrical wires together, for tying luggage zippers together so your bag does not accidentally open. Security can cut them off if they need to check the bag, but you will know the bag has been opened. A nail clipper can be used to cut them off later.
- Keep any small bags and particularly laptops between your legs

when you are checking in or making telephone calls, etc. Be especially careful with laptops since they can disappear very quickly.

- Watch your bags going through the carry-on x-ray machine and don't get distracted. Lots of laptops have disappeared when someone grabbed them while their owner was delayed going through the metal detector.

- Do not watch anyone else's luggage or carry any packages for them onto the aircraft.

- Proceed though the terminal and screening process since the boarding area is the safest area.

- Reserve an airplane seat closer to an exit. Count the number of seat rows to an exit before you buckle up. In an emergency with low visibility, you will be able to get out. Natural fabrics, such as leather or cotton, are better in a fire than synthetics, which melt sticking to the skin. Always have your shoes on when taking off and landing.

- Taking an aspirin the day before and the day of going on a long flight, especially international flights helps prevent blood clots from forming. While on board, drink lots of water, avoid alcohol and walk around every two hours.

Taxis

- Always take a licensed taxi from a taxi stand. Do not arrange transportation with someone who approaches you in the airport. These are bootleg taxis and should always be viewed with skepticism.

- If you are traveling to a foreign country, review travel guides for the most reliable travel options.

- Do not get in a taxi when there is someone in the passenger seat.

- Always sit in the back seat of the taxi.

- Do not share a taxi with anyone unless you saw them on the plane or know them well.

- Understand what the approximate fare should be before you get in the taxi. Be aware that in some locations there can be a legitimate different day and night rate (Singapore as an example).

Make sure the meter starts at zero and is on.

- Make sure you know where you are going and roughly how to get there, so you aren't given the "scenic tour."

- Look at the taxi license on the visor noting the drivers name and taxi number so that you can say, "Mr. Smith, I would like to go to (wherever it is you want to go)."

- Pay after you have gotten out of the cab with all of your belongings. There have been cases where a cab driver has been paid and then driven off with the luggage.

- Make sure you have all your bags and other possessions when you get out. You would be amazed at all the things that get left in taxi cabs. Be especially careful that you don't leave your cell phone or laptop.

Rental Cars

- After dark, have the courtesy bus drop you at your car or an employee walk you to the car.

- Get *clear* directions to where you are going.

- Consider renting a car with a global positioning system (GPS). The GPS will tell you exactly where to turn and take you right to your destination. There is normally a modest additional charge for this option.

- Walk around the car to make sure the tires are fully inflated and there are no other visible problems. Before you drive away, check where the windshield wiper controls are and how to turn on the lights. Make sure the gas tank shows full.

Hotel

- Register with your first initial only.

- 2nd to 7th floors are better in case of fire. Many fire truck ladders do not reach above the 7th floor so your risk goes up above this level. Above the 4th floor is better for preventing intruders coming from the outside. This is less of a problem if there are no balconies.

- Room access from the inside of the building rather than the outside is safer.

- Ask for a room near the elevator so you do not have to walk down long dimly lit halls.

- Have a bellhop escort you to your room and have him check the room out thoroughly, looking in the bathroom, closets, and under the bed.

- If there is a fire escape outside your window, request another room since it gives a criminal potential access to your room.

- Do not keep any valuables in your room unless they are locked up in a secure safe.

- Make sure the locks and chains on the door are working. Use a rubber door stop which you brought with you or use a chair braced under the door handle for added security.

- Put a "Do Not Disturb" sign on your door when you leave. Leave a light and the TV on in your room when you go out to make it look and sound occupied.

- Check to be sure that your windows lock and are closed correctly. In particular, check to see if there are windows in the bathroom and that they are closed.

- Always conduct your meetings in the lobby or other public area of the hotel, not your room.

- Do not flirt with the hotel staff. Remember, they have access to your room key.

- When you are dining, do not place your room key on the top of the table where the room number can be read.

- Have a flashlight with you in case of power failure. In a pinch, you can open your flip cell phone and use that as a weak source of light. Travel with a battery operated alarm clock.

- Keep the TV remote nearby since it gives you instant light and sound.

- Only open the door if you requested something and can verify it through the peep hole. If in doubt, call the front desk and question why someone is at your door.

- Ask the hotel about any local areas that should be avoided or any other issues that you should know about.

- Before you leave the hotel, take a matchbook or business card with the specific hotel address and phone number. You can use this to tell the taxi where to return. In large cities there are many hotels of the same chain and you need to know the exact one to return to.

Foreign Travel

- Learn some of the local language prior to the start of your trip. While English is really the language of the world, not everyone speaks it. You need to know some basic words to express your wants and needs. The locals will appreciate your efforts to speak their language even if you butcher it a bit. Even a few words will allow you to make friends. There is an old joke that goes, "What do you call someone who speaks two languages? Bilingual. What do you call someone who can speak three languages? Trilingual. What do you call someone who speaks only one language? American." So, learn a bit of the local language, you'll have more fun and you'll know a few words to use in an emergency.

- Use the type of passport holder that goes around the neck or waist and under your clothes to hold your passport. This is the most secure way to carry valuables. Be sure you can access that holder quickly, efficiently and without undressing. Money belts are good, but not easy to access. Velcro pockets are good because you just can't stick your fingers in there, and they are hard to get open with making noise. You can put rubber bands around a wallet to make it more difficult to get out of a pocket.

- Make two color copies of your passport and visas, one to take with you and the other to leave at home with a friend. If you lose your passport, having a copy will significantly expedite getting a new one through the nearest U.S. Embassy. Take along an extra set of passport photos. Make copies of your itinerary and airline tickets. Again, take one copy and leave one. Keep the copies you take with you in a safe, separate location. Leave a copy of the travelers checks' serial numbers with your friend.

- Check the U.S. Department of State internet site, http://www.state.gov for travel warnings regarding any of your proposed destinations. You can also call the Department of State's Office of Overseas Citizens Services from a touchtone phone at 202-647-5225. The country code for the USA is 01, so if you are dialing from an international location, you would dial 01-202-647-5225.

- Do your homework so that you understand the current political atmosphere in the areas you plan to visit. Study local maps so you understand where your hotel is in relation to the rest of the city and have a general idea of how to get around. In addition, if you look up the history and key events it will enhance your enjoyment.

- Pack a small first aid kit which includes diarrhea medication. Leave medications in their original containers, and have a doctor's written letter authorizing the use of any pain medication.

- *DO NOT* tell strangers at which hotel you are staying, no matter how nice they may seem. Even if there is no criminal intent, they may be checking to see your economic standing to charge you more on products.

- Enjoy your surroundings, but keep your eyes open at all times - look for exits, people who look shady, etc.

- When riding public transportation, sit as close as you can to the driver and with a woman whenever you possible. Try not to sit next to men in public transit. You may find that taking public transportation is safer than a single female getting in a taxi. Other times a taxi may be safer. You need to understand and be aware of the local situation.

- Keep some small change and bills readily available so you don't have to drag out the mother lode to pay for a minor item. My world traveling daughter likes to keep small change in one pocket and a few small bills in another. This way she doesn't have to drag out her neck holder and if she gets pick pocketed, they only get a small amount.

- Fold your money so that the smallest bill is on the outside.

- If you get lost, avoid pulling out the map while you are on the sidewalk. Go into a café, enjoy the local drink and plot out where you need to go. Often the proprietor or server will be happy to help you. They want you to come back again.

- Walk on the opposite side of the street from large groups of young men. No, it is not rude to cross when you see them.

- When you get off a bus, look as if you know exactly where you are going, even if you don't. First impressions are important in whether or not you will be the pegged target. Not all people will give you correct directions or instructions. Be aware there is a scam to redirect tourists to lesser known monuments or sites and in particular, shops that will provide the local referrer with a kickback. Be polite, say thank you and then go around the corner and get a second opinion.

- Use a travel agency or your hotel to secure transportation. You may wish to hire a car rather than rely on taxis. This will incur added cost, but it is safer.

- If you are getting off the beaten path, be prepared for weather extremes and carry extra items that you consider critical.

- Have a back up plan if your group gets separated, such as in crowds or getting on subways. Decide what you are going to do and where you will meet. As an example, if you get separated getting on subways, get off at the next stop, staying exactly where you get off and wait for the rest of the group to come on the next train. Since they should have gotten on at the same spot you did, when the train stops they should get off at your exact spot and you should be reunited. This comes from personal experience since I managed to get on the Metro in Paris right ahead of the rest of my family and the doors immediately slammed shut. They were on the platform and I was leaving on the train. No problem. I got off at the next stop staying exactly at the spot I got off and they arrived on the next train exactly where I was standing. Now, I will tell you we had worked out this plan what to do "if" beforehand – I just didn't think I would be the one leaving on the train.

- If you are changing money at a money exchange or ATM, pay attention to any people who are sitting around and watching. Children, as cute as they may seem, can be very adept pickpockets.

- Beware of groups of vagrant children coming up to you, since their intention may be to reach a hand into your purse, pocket or camera bag. Most children are very friendly and just wanting to talk with you, but be wary of those that come in a pack and surround you.

- Just using the manners your mother taught you - please, thank you, excuse me - and a confident attitude can get you in and out of many situations.

- Keep a matchbook or business card from your specific hotel with you so that you can show a cab driver when you want to return to the hotel. Better, have the concierge write out directions in the local language of where you want to go and return.

- Keep small bills and change with you to pay taxi drivers or other individuals. Taxi drivers are notorious for telling tourists that, no they don't have any change and will try to keep your large bill. If you are firm, they will normally come up with the change, but the easy way to avoid this is just to carry plenty of small bills. In many countries a U.S. $1 bill can be used as a tip and most of the locals can work the exchange rate faster than you can. I normally take a large number of $1 bills with me just for contingency purposes in case I run out of local small bills. I have never had them turned down. However, in an area with strong anti-American feeling, you may not want to pull out any U.S. currency.

- In any country where there is a question of security or animosity towards Americans, avoid going with a large tour group. Instead opt for your own guide since large groups make better targets.

- Avoid public demonstrations. They can turn unruly and the police can be indiscriminate in who they hit or take into custody. Worse, the crowd might turn on you, the foreigner, to take out their wrath.

- Do not look out your hotel window at public demonstrations. If there is civil unrest, stay in your hotel and contact the U.S. Embassy.

- If you are being hassled or followed try walking into a grocery store. Normal people are there and it tends to be women with children. Any woman (particularly an older woman) will know the culturally appropriate response and it is easy to interpret that situation without knowing the language. In general, people are genuinely nice and want you to feel comfortable in and appreciate their country.

- Beware of crowds since they are the favorite places for pickpockets. Watch getting on and off subways in particular. Try to avoid traveling at rush hour. A current trick is to bump into people and razor the side of the bag so that the goods fall out unnoticed. Be very alert if you are bumped in a crowd, there is a very strong possibility that someone is trying or has just picked your pocket. Another tactic is to squirt something on you and while you are being "helped" to clean up, your stuff is stolen. To make the work harder for pickpockets, walk against the crowd. While it will get you a few dirty looks, you'll probably keep your wallet. Staying out of crowds in major tourist zones will decrease your likelihood of having your pockets picked. Willie Sutton, the bank robber, was once asked why he robbed banks. His answer, "Because that's where the money is." It's the same reason that pickpockets are attracted to crowds of tourists.

- Be polite and respect local customs. Put thought into your clothing selection being sensitive to the culture and avoiding any taboos. Americans can easily be spotted by their baseball caps, shorts, clothing with large logos, and running shoes. In general, Americans are targeted because the assumption around the world is that all Americans are rich. My suggestion is don't dress in a way that screams "America".

- Americans are known for being loud, so just speak in a normal voice. Speaking louder does not help someone who doesn't understand English. Do not speak disparaging about local things saying how things are much better in the "Good ole USA." Seek the beauty and uniqueness of each destination. The locals live there every day and think it is pretty nice. Remember, it is their home!

- Be careful what you photograph. In general, do not photograph police, military, government installations, or border areas. If you are photographing people, get their permission first. Sometimes just making a gesture with your camera will get them to nod an okay. Other times they will shake their head. Do not take pictures of people that do not want to be photographed. Be very careful of taking pictures of any women, particularly in the Middle East.

- How you dress can be interpreted in very different ways around the world. What is acceptable at your local mall might only be worn at a beach in another country. Consider packing cute clothes that reach your knees, cover your shoulders and that aren't too low cut. A stole or large scarf is extremely helpful and can be used in many circumstances. More modest dress helps combat the stereotype that all American women are loose (remember, for the 4 billion people who haven't been to the US, they actually think Americans all act like the women in TV and movies... yikes!). In addition, a woman will more likely help you if you are modestly dressed.

- Go with friends when shopping. Observe all the rules for handling your purse, money and credit cards. Once again two is better than one, three better than two. A male in the group will help change the perception of the group's vulnerability.

- If you are traveling alone and feeling uncomfortable, volunteer to take a picture of a family. They will normally offer to take your picture in return and you instantly become part of that group.

- You may find yourself being touched or pinched. This is particularly true in shopping bazaars, on crowded transportation, and anywhere in crowds. Foreign males sometimes treat this almost as a game. Depending on the level of the attention, your choices are to ignore it or say something. If you know some of the language you can say loudly, "Leave me alone," "Shame," or "Enough." If you don't know the local language, use your language, he'll get the idea. You can also talk to a nearby local older man or woman saying, "Aunt/Uncle, this man is bothering me." Since most cultures do not want to lose face, they will normally intervene and scold the man. After you've made a remark to let him know that it is not acceptable, move on and don't exacerbate the situation. Don't be surprised if the pincher just laughs. If a male is with you, try to keep him close behind you. Keep the younger girls to the middle of a group since they will be the most obvious targets. Watch out for crowds and move away from problem areas as quickly as possible.

- Stay sober. If you get drunk or drink to excess, you become a very easy target. Many foreign men have the stereotype idea that American women are loose and free. Do nothing that supports that idea. While you personally may not be affected, the next American woman that comes along may be.

- Do not go anywhere alone with young men even, if they promise to take you to "the best disco in town."

- Drive the type of cars that are used locally. Your objective is not to stand out from the rest of the population. Keeping the windows rolled up will prevent someone from reaching in and stealing your purse when you stop at an intersection. Don't give rides to strangers.

- If you rent a car know the directions and be very wary if you have mechanical problems. One scam involves puncturing a tire as you leave the airport and then two "Good Samaritans" show up to help you change the tire. One helps you while the other one helps himself to your purse and anything else available.

- Try not to drive at night. In some countries the roads are not good, the cars are not well maintained, and lights seem to be optional. It is not worth the risk.

- You may encounter roadblocks where your papers will be checked carefully. This happens more often in Africa, South America and communist or formerly communist countries. Stay calm and be patient.

- Drive extra carefully since penalties for infractions can be severe, particularly if you are involved in an accident with a fatality. Know the local laws.

- Your biggest danger with overseas travel is being involved in an automobile accident, therefore take extra care when driving or deciding on transportation. You may wish to buy additional short term medical and medical evacuation insurance before you leave if you are planning to visit less developed countries or are planning on getting off the beaten path. The medical facilities in some countries are less than desired and you will want to get to better facilities as soon as possible.

- Carry plenty of hand sanitizer since clean restroom facilities are not always available. An extra pack of tissues might be handy.

- Don't try to fight robbers. Give them the money. You may wish to carry a money clip or other small packet of money to relinquish.

- Leave your good jewelry at home. You may wish to have costume jewelry and a cheap watch that you don't mind losing. I am aware of at least one case where a woman and her sister were sitting in a car in broad daylight at a crowded intersection in Mexico City when a criminal walked up, stuck a gun though the open window, and demanded the sister's $1,000 watch. I have also heard of criminals coming by in other countries on motor scooters and grabbing watches off of women who were casually resting their arm on the open window of their car.

- If you are traveling in known hazardous areas, you may wish to hire armed guards or there may be caravans with armed escorts going from one city to the next. Sometimes the local police can be hired as extra guards. Decide if you want them in a separate car or with you.

- If you are traveling by overnight train, lock the compartment door. Try to have one member of the group stay awake on guard. Rotate this duty every two hours. Overnight trains are notorious for having criminals come through and steal valuables while the victim is sleeping.

- If you feel uncomfortable and are with another female friend, feel free to link arms. This is rarely done in the US, but is quite common in other countries. It makes you look less American and in most places, more local. It also expresses that you are already with a friend and aren't looking for a new one.

- With all the concern about child abductions now, if you are traveling alone with your child make sure you have documentation proving that it is your child and you have right to travel. As an example, make a copy of both your and your spouse's passports on the same piece of paper. Have your spouse write a "to whom it may concern" letter stating that he gives you and the child permission to travel to these countries on these dates. Make sure it is signed, notarized, and the signature can be compared with the passport copy. If your spouse is deceased, make sure to take a copy of the death certificate with you. Get a passport for your child as soon as you can.

- Be very careful about buying antiquities. First, they are probably fakes and second many countries require an export permit for antiquities, particularly Turkey, Egypt and Mexico.

- Don't use drugs or try to smuggle them into your destination. Foreign countries can have severe penalties including death for carrying drugs. Even with a lesser penalty, you do not want to spend any time in a foreign jail. It will not be a pleasant experience.

- If you do lose your passport or have other legal problems, go immediately to the nearest US Embassy or Consulate. The Embassy or Consulate personnel will be very helpful but remember, *you are in a foreign country and are subject to their laws*. Be polite and PATIENCE will be necessary.

Terrorism

The reality in today's environment is that Americans are not loved throughout the world. While most of the locals that you encounter will like Americans there is a faction of people that have strong anti-American views. You need to understand this and take the proper precautions.

- Check US State Department warnings at www.state.gov before you leave.

- Try not to dress like an American. Leave your T-shirts that have USA, the American flag, your college or other clearly American logo at home. Many Americans seem to be walking billboards with all their various slogans, logos, and name brands. Leave your white running shoes at home. In general, dress in darker colors and more sedately than you normally would, particularly for Europe and the Middle East.

- Get a plain cover for your passport. No reason to advertise you are an American. Memorize your passport number so you don't have to pull out your passport when you are filling out your landing card.

- Don't readily volunteer that you are an American on the street. You may wish to adopt the persona of a Swiss, South African, Canadian or other nationality when asked where you came from by the local shopkeeper or taxi driver. I will tell you however, that a lot of shopkeepers are extremely adept at recognizing your country of origin. I met one young shopkeeper in Cairo that spoke a smattering of seventeen languages and correctly identified nine different nationalities as they were walking by. He told me what his guess was and then addressed them in their native language to verify their nationality. By the way, he missed on me because I was not dressed like a typical American.

- Keep a low profile and try not to draw attention to yourself.

- Avoid places where lots of Americans hang out. These are potential targets.

- Do not go into areas where it is likely there will be a strong negative opinion of Americans or foreigners. An example would be some ethnic neighborhoods or villages. If you sense that you are not welcome, *leave immediately.*

- Avoid crowds of tourists. Large groups present desirable targets for terrorists who are trying to make the largest impact with whatever they do

- Travel in smaller groups. In some localities it may be better to rent a taxi or hire a car with a guide than travel on a tour bus if foreigners are being targeted. Some tours buses have been specifically targeted because of the large number of tourists on board.

- Whenever possible, have your hotel or a reputable travel agency, arrange your transportation.

- If you have to hail a taxi on the street, select it at random. Keep the windows rolled up to within 2 inches of the top so somebody can not reach into the taxi for your purse or packages, and nothing can get tosscd into the taxi.

- Be alert to unattended bags/packages. Report these to authorities.

- Refuse any unexpected packages that someone tries to give you or that show up at your hotel room. Be very wary of any letter that is thick, of suspicious origin, has misspelled words, has a strange smell, grease stains, bad handwriting in block letters, is unbalanced (one end of the letter is much heavier than the other), has unusual weight, or has a small hole in the package that may have been used for the arming device or safety pin.

- Beware of loitering people. Look out your hotel window before leaving to see if there appears to be surveillance. If the same utility truck or other vehicle keeps appearing, it might indicate a problem.

- Do not accept any food or drink from strangers since it might contain organisms your body is not used to or worse, it could be drugged. In the same manner, be careful about strangers insisting you go to a restaurant you had not planned to go to since the food might contain something you don't want. Don't let politeness overcome good judgment.

- Trust your sixth sense. If something doesn't seem right, it may not be, so get out or leave.

- Know where safe locations are. I define these as hotels, police and fire stations. As you are walking or driving around pay attention to these locations so that you know where to go in an emergency or if you need help.

- Try to vary the times and routes of your travel. Be especially careful in the morning since it is usually easier to predict leaving times than what time you might return.

- Do not leave any business papers in your hotel room. These might identify you as a valuable target and also commercial espionage is rampant in some parts of the world.

- Make sure the transportation you selected is in good mechanical condition. If not, get out and select another cab. You do not want to be broken down in the wrong neighborhood.

- If you are driving a car, check to make sure there are no loose wires or anything else unusual. Keep the windows rolled up. This will help prevent unwanted packages (grenades or bombs) from being dropped into your car.

- Understand where the choke points (places where you may come to a stop) are on your route and pay particular attention to these areas. Be prepared to take evasive action.

- If you are someplace and shooting occurs, immediately drop to the floor. Try to get behind some furniture or other protection and stay there. If you stand up, you are more likely to be shot. Remember, law enforcement personnel are making split second life and death decisions. Don't be involved in that decision process, stay down. DO NOT PICK UP A GUN. The bad guys know you are not one of them and law enforcement will think you're one of the bad guys. In that situation it is likely both groups will shoot at you. Be aware that police may toss in stun grenades, which cause bright flashes and painful bangs. Continue to stay on floor and do not get up. After the shooting stops, you may be treated roughly by the police until they can sort out who the bad guys are and who you are. Stay calm and be patient while they get their job done.

Hostage

After trying to avoid being involved in an "adverse situation" using all the methods described above, you still may find yourself in the difficult position of being captured and taken hostage. As terrifying as it is to be taken hostage, the first thing to remember is that they want you for a reason or they would have already disposed of you. Recognize that people will be looking for you and trying to secure your release. You should be aware that U.S. policy is firmly committed to resisting terrorist blackmail. This means they will not pay money for your release or make any other concessions. This does not mean that will not talk with your captors or try to secure your release. They will work diligently to help secure your release. They just will not make any concessions in the belief that it would encourage future hostage takers.

If you are taken hostage by a terrorist group:

- Don't be a hero. Do not make any sudden movements.
- Follow orders precisely. Calm down and get yourself under control.
- Keep a low profile and avoid eye contact.
- Don't volunteer information. Cooperate passively.
- If you do have discussions with guards, discuss family as a common topic to build rapport. Do not discuss politics.
- Keep a daily routine. Play mental games to stay alert.
- Eat what you are given even though it may not be appetizing or food you would normally eat. You will need your strength and you do not know how long it will take for you to be released or rescued.
- Evaluate carefully if it appears there is an opportunity to escape. Make sure there is a high probability of success. It is one thing if you are in a city and your guards fall asleep. It is a different thing when your guards fall asleep and you are in the middle of the jungle with no food and uncertain of which direction to go. Make sure there is a high probability of success, because if you are

recaptured, you will most likely suffer a beating or worse.

- Maintain a positive attitude. Again, remember that you have value to your captors, that's why they grabbed you. Remember also that people will be looking for you and trying to get you released or rescued.

- If it becomes apparent that the terrorists are on a suicide mission, such as United 93 on September 11, 2001, you need to make the decision to prevent the terrorists from hitting their larger main target. Gather as many other hostages as you can and do whatever you can to thwart their plans. If you are going to die no matter what, then die trying your very best to help save others. This is a very difficult situation, but the gratitude of those you save will be everlasting.

Let's review **Travel**:

- ✓ Prepare before you leave.
- ✓ Take direct flights and minimize luggage.
- ✓ Only use licensed taxis.
- ✓ Register with first initial and be escorted to your room when checking in.
- ✓ Make sure all locks are in good working order.
- ✓ Learn some of the local language before leaving for foreign travel.
- ✓ Check with the US State Department for travel warnings.
- ✓ Do not dress like an American.
- ✓ Have a back up plan if your group gets separated.
- ✓ Be polite.
- ✓ Behave yourself and drink in moderation.
- ✓ Try to avoid large crowds of tourists in areas of unrest.
- ✓ Have the hotel or reputable travel agency arrange your transportation.
- ✓ Try to vary your times and routes.
- ✓ If shooting does occur, immediately go to the floor.
- ✓ In a hostage situation try to remain calm and recognize there will be people working for your release.
- ✓ If it's a suicide mission, do your best to prevent it.

Chapter 11

Identity Theft Prevention

I dentity theft is the number one consumer fraud and the fastest growing crime today. There are an estimated 10 million identity thefts per year. Every day we hear a new story about a company misplacing the personal information of millions of people. In some cases, it is an honest mistake and the data is safe, but in other cases the data gets into the hands of criminals. If you suffer identity theft, it will require some time and effort to get it resolved.

Let's discuss the things you can do to prevent the theft of your identity.

- Guard your social security number zealously. Do not give it out unless absolutely necessary.

- Use a cross cut shredder on all the discarded documents or papers containing personal information. Criminals routinely go through trash to retrieve credit card slips, bank statements and other personal information. This is sometimes referred to as dumpster diving. Don't let any of your personal information leave intact via your trash can.

- Don't give any personal information out on the telephone or your computer unless you initiated the contact.

- Don't participate in telephone surveys. Criminals are very clever at getting confidential information from you.

- If someone calls and claims to be from the bank, credit card company, etc. and giving you your account number, but wanting you to verify the correctness by you stating your password or mother's maiden name, get their name and telephone number stating that you will call them back. Do not call that number back, but call the published telephone number of that institution and check to see if there are questions about your account. Put a fraud alert on that account.

- Do not respond to emails that look like they come from your bank or other business requesting you to update or verify your account number, password, mother's maiden name or social security number. Criminals have gotten very clever about making it look like a legitimate request from your bank with logos and everything. This is called "phishing." They are trying to get personal information from you. Do not click on any links or respond to it. Call the bank or other business to inquire as to the validity of the transmission and thereby alerting all parties if it is fraudulent. You can also forward the phishing spam to www.spam@uce.gov. In the midst of writing this book, we received a bogus email from a bank requesting personal information. We followed the steps above and when the bank was called they thanked us and stated they were turning it over to their fraud department.

- Do not open email attachments unless you know the sender since they may contain spyware or other software that might be used to capture personal information. Make sure you have a good security system in place that provides for virus scanning and a firewall. Some very good free spyware detection software is available at www.spybot.info. While it is free, I suggest you make a donation if you decide to use it.

- Do not use the same password for everything. If criminals get the password they will have access to everything. Use letters, numbers and symbols in your password making it more difficult to guess.

- Verify any website you assume to be secure has the "s" added to the http:// address so it should read **https://.** You will find this toward the top of your screen in the address line. Double check that it is the address of the site you intended to access. You can check the padlock icon, often found at the right hand bottom of your screen, to verify it is closed thereby indicating a secure site.

- If you have a wireless network in your home, make sure you have security software in place to prevent your neighbors from reading all of your messages.

- Carefully check your bank and credit card monthly statements to verify they contain no unusual activities.
- Get a credit rating statement once a year and review it carefully.
- There are monitoring services available that will advise you any time someone checks your credit rating and who they were. This can help prevent an unauthorized person from trying to get a credit card or other financial transaction.
- Never put your social security number on your checks or as your driver's license number. Some states use the social security number on driver's licenses, but you should request a different number to be used on your license. Most states honor this request.
- Put outgoing mail in a U.S. Postal mail box. Do not put it in your mail box with the red flag up for that signals criminals there is something to steal.
- Don't keep personal information on your laptop. A significant number of laptops are stolen each year. Don't give criminals a bonus by having personal information on the laptop they have just grabbed.
- If you discard a computer make sure you clean off the hard drive. It is not enough just to delete the files; the hard drive must be really cleaned to prevent someone restoring the data. There are software programs that will do this very effectively.
- Make a color copy of the front and back of your credit cards. Keep the copies in a safe place, like a safety deposit box. In case the cards are lost you will have the information to contact the companies in order to cancel the cards and inform them of the loss.
- Carry the minimum number of credit cards with you and cancel those cards that you really do not use.
- If your purse or credit cards are stolen take the following actions:
  1. File a police report.
  2. Cancel credit cards – you have the numbers from your color copies.
  3. Call the three national credit reporting organizations to place a fraud alert on your name and social security number.
     - Equifax 1-800-525-6285
     - Experian 1-888-397-3742
     - Trans Union 1-800-680-7289

4. Contact the Social Security Administration's fraud line: 1-800-269-0271

- Check with your homeowners insurance about adding a rider regarding identity theft. Some insurance companies are offering this rider at a modest cost.
- The Federal Trade Commission has very good information about identity theft at www.consumer.gov/idtheft. You can also file a complaint at www.ftc.gov or call toll free 877-382-4357.

Let's review **Identity Theft**:

✓ Guard your social security number.
✓ Don't give out any personal information unnecessarily.
✓ Do not respond to unsolicited email or telephone requests for personal information.
✓ Check monthly credit card statements carefully.
✓ Request and review your credit rating report each year.

Chapter 12

Self-Defense Training and Martial Arts

ny training you get in self-defense is good, and obviously some is better than others. Try to find classes that are focused on techniques women can do. A great technique is no good if it is too complicated or requires the strength and agility of a 20-year-old male. They must be techniques that the average woman can deliver and achieve good results. There are some very good classes in which you practice on padded opponents therefore allowing you to go at 100% attack mode.

If you desire to take martial arts training, decide what your objectives are. Check to make sure the instruction and classes coincide with your objectives. Visit the school; see who is training, and try to ascertain the level of competence of the instruction. How long have they been in business? Are they only focused on advancing students quickly? I refer to these as belt factories and they are to be avoided. Do they have specific women's self-defense training? What level of physical contact is normal? Some schools have light contact sparring and others have full contact. Are they focused primarily on the sport aspects? Several of the martial arts are now Olympic sports. These might be fine for the individual that wants to compete, but they typically have rigid rules about where to kick or hit and therefore may not teach you realistic street self-defense. As an example, Tae Kwon Do rules do not allow you to kick to the knees, groin or punch to the face - all places I suggest you target. Ask around and talk to people about the various schools located near you. The competence of the instructor is very important. Make sure there are other female students. Observe how they are being treated and talk with several of them. The school should be reasonably close making it easier for you to attend more often. The more routine your training, the more proficient you will become. There may be some schools in your area that have specific self-defense classes and if so, check them out.

There are a many different styles and variations of martial arts. Consider these general categories of schools as a starting point.

Start with this group	Other styles to consider
Aikido	Tae Kwon Do
Hapkido	Kick Boxing
Karate	Ju Jitsu
Kung Fu	Judo

Aikido is placed at the top of my list for several reasons. First, it is an excellent self-defense art which redirects the energy of the attacker and therefore doesn't require lots of strength or muscle, making it a good choice for women. Second, the philosophy of aikido is to only use the minimum force necessary to deal with an attacker which aligns it with self-defense laws.

Whichever martial art you select, if you achieve a high skill level, such as a black belt, you will be a formidable opponent.

Training in martial arts will give you further understanding of self-defense, but there are other benefits as well. You will gain confidence, increased flexibility and stamina, speed, better balance, and improved coordination. Many of the martial arts also include cultural aspects in their training. Whichever classes you choose, you should have a good workout and enjoy training with that particular group.

Let's review **Self-Defense Training and Martial Arts**:

✓ Match your objectives with the style, specific type of instruction and school.
✓ Any martial art training will probably be beneficial.

Conclusion

This book covers many areas and has lots of ideas for improving your and your family's personal safety. It can be the basis or framework for a personal safety plan. You must make the ideas you select part of your everyday life. Live the 4 A's. I encourage you to continue practicing with someone to remain familiar with the physical self-defense techniques. The techniques should become second nature so they are a natural response and not something you have to think about. Just by reading this book you have become more aware of ways to reduce your risks, and if necessary, how to successfully handle a confrontation with an attacker.

My deepest wish is that the things you have learned from this book will allow you and your family to journey through life safely.

Your thoughts or suggestions regarding this book and any personal experiences you wish to share would be much appreciated. Please go to the www.livingsafelytoday.com website and go to the contact page to submit your comments or email them to fred@livingsafelytoday.com.

Appendix A

General Self–Defense Guidelines

T he laws of your state give you a fundamental right to defend yourself and others. While state laws do vary, they tend to be increasingly consistent with the Model Penal Code (MPC) which, while not law and has no binding effect, is a comprehensive revision of the criminal code. MPC §3.04(1) states; "A person is justified in using force upon another person if he believes that such force is immediately necessary to protect himself against the exercise of unlawful force by the other on the present occasion." Similarly, the Texas State Penal Code (TPC) § 9.31 (a) states; "a person is justified in using force against another when and to the degree he reasonably believes the force is immediately necessary to protect himself against the other's use or attempted use of unlawful force."

In general, the principles and laws concerning of self-defense are similar, but can be confusing. This is my (non-lawyer) synopsis of the laws and should ***not be construed as legal advice***, but some general understanding regarding self-defense legalities might be helpful. You should research and be familiar with your own specific state and local laws.

The law generally takes a dim view of using force anytime, since at the least, it's a breach of the peace. There are issues regarding whether you might be breaking the law and whether you may be subject to civil or criminal penalties. Just because you are not charged with a crime does not mean you might not be subject to a civil lawsuit. Law enforcement will be looking at any incident to determine what happened and was reasonable force used. Defendant's lawyers will recast the events into the most favorable version for their client, and witnesses get amnesia. The laws are complex and yet, they can sometimes be vague. What are the laws with regard to protecting yourself in common-speak as opposed to legalize?

My advice is to do everything reasonable to avoid having to demonstrate your self-defense skills. Run, if you can, or use verbal self-defense. However, if avoidance is impossible, and you are being attacked, then you have the right to defend yourself and others (children, parents, even strangers) to the *lawful extent.*

Generally:

- You cannot respond to verbal aggression with force.
- You cannot invoke self-defense if you provoked or encouraged aggression. As an example, if you agree to go outside to fight, you cannot claim self-defense.
- You cannot use force against a threat in the future ("If you do that again, I'll hit you."). The threat must be immediate.
- You do not have to wait to be struck, but the threat of imminent attack must be there. Once the threat is made and someone is preparing to attack, such as drawing back their arm to punch, you may begin your defense.
- You may respond to force with equal or slightly greater force. The amount of force used must be reasonable.
- You may use deadly force to prevent the loss of possessions only in very limited circumstances.
- You may use deadly force if you reasonably believe your life or a third party's life is in danger or great bodily harm will result. The MPC § 3.04 (2)b sets forth conditions when deadly force is justified; when the defendant believes that such force is immediately necessary to protect himself against: death, serious bodily injury, forcible rape, or kidnapping. State laws do differ – as an example, TPC § 9.32(3) B adds robbery and aggravated robbery as justification for the use of deadly force in addition to the four reasons previously mentioned.
- You may not use deadly force if you have a reasonable chance of

getting to complete safety by retreating, except there is generally no requirement to retreat in your dwelling or place of work.

- You may reasonably believe the attacker has a weapon if he tells you he does and acts accordingly, even though he doesn't display it. A deadly weapon can be a knife or gun, but it can also be a screwdriver, baseball bat, scissors, vase or any other instrument that could be used to potentially cause death.

- As soon as the attacker stops his attack, retreats, or is incapacitated, you must cease any further use of force on him.

- If the attacker strikes you and then immediately stops, offering no further threat, you may not retaliate, because then by definition, you become the attacker.

- Your home is your castle. In your home, you may use deadly force to prevent violent entry, an attack on your person, or to stop criminal intruders believed intent upon committing a felony. Most states do not require that you retreat as far as you can before employing deadly force. You should tell the intruder to stop unless you believe the request would endanger your or others lives or be useless.

This is not intended to be legal advice, but rather a very simplistic synopsis of the various complex laws regarding self-defense. You must be familiar with your own specific state and local laws. You may wish to seek the advice of an attorney for further understanding.

Appendix B

U.S. Department of Justice Bureau of Justice 2004 Crime Statistics

U.S. residents 12 and older experienced 24 million crimes.

77% (18.6 million) were property crimes
21% (5.2 million) were violent crime

70% of female rape or sexual assault victims stated offender was intimate, relative, friend or acquaintance.

62% of males and 45% of females stated individual(s) who robbed them were strangers. (Note - 55% of the time the female knew who the robber was.)

51% of incidents happened from 6 a.m. to 6 p.m.

65% of rapes or sexual assaults happened from 6 p.m. to 6 a.m. 8% of the time a weapon was used during a rape or sexual assault.

25% of crime was at or near the victim's home.
15% was on streets that were not close to the home.
14% was at school.
 8% occurred in commercial establishments.

22% of the time a weapon was used during the commission of a violent crime.

43% of the time a murder victim was related to or acquainted with their assailants.

67% of victims who suffered violence by an intimate (current or former spouse, boyfriend, girlfriend) reported alcohol was a factor.

Other statistics can be accessed at the Federal Bureau of Investigations website www.fbi.gov. The FBI publishes the data in the Uniform Crime Reporting (UCR) Program.

Appendix C

Resources

Aikido

Aikido Association of America
1016 Belmont Avenue
Chicago, Illinois 60657
773-525-3141
www.aaa-aikido.com
Executive Director: Steven Toyota

The Woodlands Aikido Center
1045 Pruitt Road
Spring, Texas 77380
832-298-6453
www.aikidocenter.com
Sensei Michael Black

Three Rivers Aikido
7403 Manchester Road
Maplewood, Missouri 63143
314-645-2345
www.threeriversaikido.com
Sensei Elliot Freeman

Children

National Center for Missing and Exploited Children
Charles B. Wang International Children's Building
699 Prince Street
Alexandria, Virginia 22314
1-800-THE-LOST
www.missingkids.com

Credit Reporting Organizations

Equifax
PO Box 740241
Atlanta, Georgia 30374
For credit report 800-685-1111
For fraud 800-525-6285

Experian
PO Box 2002
Allen, Texas 75013
For credit report or fraud 888-397-3742

Trans Union
PO Box 1000
Chester, Pennsylvania 19022
For credit report 800-888-4213
For fraud 800-680-7289

Crime

U.S. Department of Justice
950 Pennsylvania Avenue NW
Washington D.C. 20530
202-514-2000
www.usdoj.gov

The National Crime Prevention Council
1000 Connecticut Avenue NW
13th Floor
Washington D.C. 20036
202-466-6272
www.ncpc.org

Domestic Violence

Break the Cycle
P.O. Box 64996
Los Angles, California 90064
888-988-TEEN
www.breakthecycle.org

National Domestic Violence Hotline
P.O. Box 161810
Austin, TX 78716
1-800-799-SAFE
www.ndcv.org

National Coalition Against Domestic Violence
P.O. Box 18749
Denver, CO 80218
303-839-1852
www.ncadv.org

Department of Justice
Violence Against Women Office
www.ojp.usdoj.gov/vawo

Drugs
U.S. Department of Justice
Drug Enforcement Administration
Mailstop: AES
2401 Jefferson Davis Highway
Alexandria, Virginia 22301
www.dea.gov

Elderly
National Center on Elder Abuse
1201 15th Street NW, Suite 350
Washington, D.C. 20005
202-898-2586
www.elderabusecenter.org

Firearms Training
National Rifle Association
11250 Waples Mill Road
Fairfax, Virginia 22030
www.nra.org

Foreign Travel
U.S. Department of State
2201 C Street NW
Washington, D.C. 20520
General information 202-647-4000
Travel information 202-647-5225
www.state.gov

Identity Theft
Federal Trade Commission
600 Pennsylvania Avenue, NW
Washington, D.C. 20580
202-326-2222
www.consumer.gov/idtheft/
See also: Credit Reporting Organizations

Rape and Sexual Assault
Rape, Abuse, and Incest National Network
635-B Pennsylvania Ave., SE
Washington, D.C. 20003
1-800-656-HOPE
www.rainn.org

U.S. Department of Justice
National Sex Offender Public Registry
www.nsopr.gov

National Coalition Against Sexual Assault
912 North Second Street
Harrisburg, PA 17102
717-232-7460

National Sexual Violence Resource Center
123 North Enola Drive
Enola, Pennsylvania 17025
877-739-3895
www.nsvrc.org

U.S. Department of Justice
Office on Violence Against Women
800 K Street NW, Suite 920
Washington, D.C. 20530
202-307-6026
www.ojp.usdoj.gov

Sex Offender Public Registry
National Sex Offender Public Registry
U.S. Department of Justice
www.nsopr.gov

Social Security Administration
Social Security Administration
Office of Public Inquiries
Windsor Park Building
6401 Security Blvd.
Baltimore, Maryland 21235
Fraud line: 800-269-0271
www.socialsecurity.gov

Stalking
Aware
P.O. Box 242
Bedford, Maryland 01730-0242
1-877-67-AWARE
www.aware.org

Victim Assistance
National Center for Victims of Crime
2000 M Street NW, Suite 480
Washington, D.C. 20036
202-467-8700
www.ncvc.org

National Victim Center
2111 Wilson Blvd. Suite 300
Arlington, Virginia 22201
800-FYI-CALL
703-276-2880
www.nal.usda.gov
Email: nvc@mail.nvc.gov

Office for Victims of Crime Resource Center
National Criminal Justice Reference Service
U.S. Department of Justice
P.O. Box 6000
Rockville, MD 20849
800-851-3420
www.ojp.gov.ovcres/welcome

National Organization for Victim Assistance
510 King Street, Suite 424
Alexandria, Virginia 22314
800-TRY-NOVA
www.trynova.org

Bibliography

Berry, Dawn Bradley. *The Domestic Violence Sourcebook – Everything You Need To Know,* Los Angles, California: Lowell House, 1995

Black, Henry Campbell, Nolan, Joseph R., Nolan-Haley, Jacqueline M. *Black's Law Dictionary,* St. Paul, Minnesota: West Publishing Co. 1990

Chaiet, Donna. *Staying Safe While Shopping,* New York: The Rosen Publishing Group Inc., 1995

Chaiet, Donna. *Staying Safe at Home,* New York: The Rosen Publishing Group, Inc., 1995

Cho, Sihak Henry. *Tae Kwon Do – Secrets of Korean Karate,* Singapore: Charles E. Tuttle Company, 1968

Coleman, Marlene M. *Safe & Sound Healthy Travel with Children,* Guilford, Connecticut: The Globe Pequot Press, 2003

Consumer Reports: *A Quick Exit From Locked Trunks,* April 2006

Cope, Carol Soret. *Stranger Danger – How to Keep Your Child Safe,* New York: Cader Books, 1997

Cornell State University. www.law.cornell.edu/statutes.html

Davis, Barry. *SAS Self Defense,* Glasgow, UK, Harper Collins, 1999

De Becker, Gavin. *Protecting the Gift,* New York: The Dial Press, 1999

Department of State. *A Safe Trip Abroad,* Bureau of Consular Affairs Publication 10942, March 2002

Dillman, George and Thomas, Chris. *Advanced Pressure Point Grappling,* Reading, Pennsylvania: George Dillman Karate International, 1995

Dyer, Gerri. *Safe, Smart, and Self Reliant – Personal Safety for Women and Children,* Rockville, Maryland: Safety Press, 1996

Federal Bureau of Investigation. *A Parent's Guide to Internet Safety,* Washington D.C.

Findlaw. www.findlaw.com/casecode/

Finkelhor, David, Mitchell, Kimberly and Wolak, Janis. *Highlights of the Youth Internet safety Survey,* Washington, D.C.: U.S. Department of Justice, 2001

Fisher, Bonnie S., Cullen, Francis T., and Turner, Michael G. *The Sexual Victimization of College Women,* Washington D.C.: U.S. Department of Justice, Bureau of Justice Statistics, and National Institute of Justice, 2000

Harman, Patricia. *The Danger Zone,* Parkside, Illinois: Parkside Publishing, 1992

Kelly, Kate. *The Complete Guide to Family Preparedness: Living in an Unsafe World,* New York: New American Library, 2000

'Lectric Law Library. www.lectlaw.com/def/do30.htm

Legal Definitions. www.legal-definitions.com

Lindquist, Scott. *The Date Rape Prevention Book-The Essential Guide for Girls and Women,* Naperville, Illinois: Sourcebooks, Inc., 2000

McNab, Chris and Rabiger, Joanna. *The Personal Security Handbook,* Guilford, Connecticut: The Lyons Press, 2003

Metakasa, Tanya K. *Safe Not Sorry,* New York: Harper Collins Publishers, 1997

Motley, James B. *Protect Yourself, Your Family, Your Home,* McLean, Virginia: Brassey's (US), 1994

National Crime Prevention Council and the National Safety Council. *Alone Behind the Wheel*

National Crime Prevention Council and the Overland Park Kansas Police Department. *Keeping Kids Safe – Kids Keeping Safe,* 1993

National Drug Intelligence Center and George Mason University, *Drug Facilitated Sexual Assault Resource Guide,* May, 2003

Nawanna, Gladson I. *Traveling Abroad Post "9-11" & In The Wake of Terrorism,* Baltimore, MD: Frontline Publishers, 2004

Perkins, John, Ridenhour, Al, Kovsky, Matt. *Attack Proof –The Ultimate Guide to Personal Protection,* Human Kinetics, 2000

Sampson, Rana. *Acquaintance Rape of College Students,* Washington D.C.: U.S. Department of Justice, Office of Community Oriented Policing Services, 2002

Shaw, Scott. *Hapkido – Korean Art of Self-Defense,* Singapore: Charles E. Tuttle Company, 1996

Shaw, Scott. *The Tao of Self-Defense,* York Beach, Maine: Samuel Weisner, Inc., 2000

State and local governments on the net. www.statelocalgov.net/index.cfm/

Tjaden, Patricia and Thoennes, Nancy. *Stalking in America: Findings From the National Violence Against Women Survey,*National Institute of Justice and Center For Disease Control, 1998

U.S. Department of Justice Drug Enforcement Administration, *Ecstasy and Predatory Drugs,* February 2003

U.S. Department of Justice. *Drugs of Abuse,* 2005 Edition

Weaver, Scott. *Silent Resolve - A Collection of Personal Protection Options for Women,* Chesterfield, Missouri, 1995

Willis, Donna K. and Morris, Bruce C. *Keep Safe - 101 Ways to Enhance Your Safety and Protect Your Family,* Alameda, California: Hunter House Publishers, 2000

Winkler, Kathleen. *Date Rape – A Hot Issue,* Berkeley Heights, New Jersey: Enslow Publisher Inc., 1995

Wooden, Kenneth. *Child Lures – What Every Parent and Child Should Know About Preventing Sexual Abuse and Abduction,* Arlington, Texas: The Summit Publishing Group, 1995

Wright, Cynthia. *Everything You Need to Know About Dealing With Stalking,* New York, Rosen Publishing Group Inc., 2000

Yamada, Yoshimitsu and Pimsler, Steven. *Ultimate Aikido – Secrets of Self-Defense and Inner Power,* Secaucus, New Jersey: Carol Publishing Group, 1996

Index

throat choke:
    front, 62-63, 69-70, 75-77   one
    arm , 80-82
Trans Union, 161, 174

U

U.S. Department of Justice, 3, 109,
    123, 129, 171, 175-177
U.S. Department of State, 146, 175

V

verbal self-defense, 38-39

W

walking, 22-25
wrists grabbed, 48-61
wrist release, 48-50
wrist lock turn, 51-63

About the Author

Fred Vogt, a husband and the father of three daughters, has a passion about women remaining safe while going about their daily lives. Although he studied martial arts for years in aikido and tae kwon do, achieving multiple black belts, it was not until after he left the corporate world that he was able to devote his energies to teaching women about their personal safety. He developed the 4 A's to Women's Personal Safety curriculum and has taught this class widely in local, college and international settings. This book incorporates those concepts that he teaches in class.

See Sally Kick Ass DVD

A DVD covering the physical self-defense techniques mentioned in this book is available through www.livingsafelytoday.com or www.seesallykickass.com. This DVD goes into more detail concerning exactly how to apply the various techniques by showing them in both regular and slow motion. It will help you understand the various self-defense techniques illustrated in this book. You can log onto the websites for more information.

LaVergne, TN USA
02 September 2010
195445LV00001B/66/A